In
Good
Conscience

Jossey-Bass books and products are available through most bookstores. To contact Jossey-Bass directly, call (888) 378-2537, fax to (800) 605-2665, or visit our website at www.josseybass.com.

Substantial discounts on bulk quantities of Jossey-Bass books are available to corporations, professional associations, and other organizations. For details and discount information, contact the special sales department at Jossey-Bass.

For sales outside the United States, please contact your local Simon & Schuster International Office.

Text design by Joseph Piliero.

 Manufactured in the United States of America on Lyons Falls Turin Book. This paper is acid-free and 100 percent totally chlorine-free.

Library of Congress Cataloging-in-Publication Data
Runkle, Anna, 1963–
   In good conscience : a practical, emotional, and spiritual guide to deciding whether to have an abortion / Anna Runkle. — 1st ed.
    p. cm.
   Includes bibliographical references and index.
   ISBN 0-7879-4149-2 (cloth : alk. paper)   *165*
   1. Abortion. 2. Pregnancy, Unwanted—Decision making. I. Title.
  HQ767.R86 1998
  363.46—ddc21
                                                 98-25319
                                                 CIP

FIRST EDITION
PB Printing   10 9 8 7 6 5 4 3 2 1

In
Good
Conscience

*A Practical, Emotional,
and Spiritual Guide
to Deciding Whether to Have
an Abortion*

Anna Runkle

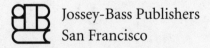

Jossey-Bass Publishers
San Francisco

For my beloved
Dennis Woulf
1967–1997

Contents

Acknowledgments

I wish to thank all the friends, family, and associates whose kindness and support made this book possible, and to extend special gratitude to the following people: Bill Azevedo, Esteban Azevedo, Lianne Davis, Rev. Tom Davis, Rory Darrah, Jacqueline Deaver-Celenza, Sheryl Fullerton, Margie King, Will Lopes, Ken Lupoff, David MacLeod, Debbie MacLeod, Peter MacLeod, Michelle McKeegan, Andy Pasternack, Rachel Petty, Patrick Ridge, Carol Robb, Rev. Peter Rose, Kirsten Runkle, Déjà Shepherd, Kevin Shepherd, Katie Simon, Grete Stenersen, Rebecca Whiteman, the good people of Desert House of Prayer, the National Abortion Federation, the National Abortion Rights Action League, Planned Parenthood Federation of America (particularly Gloria, Barbara, Jon, and Helena), the Religious Coalition for Reproductive Rights, my friends and colleagues at the PPFA San Francisco Office, and the women who shared their own abortion stories out of love for the readers of this book.

I would also like to express my thanks to my mother and father, Barbara Azevedo and Bret Runkle, as well as W. R. Page and my Grandmarie who are not here to see the publication of this book but whose love, encouragement, and belief in me have endured.

A. R.

The Author

Anna Runkle is a consultant for Planned Parenthood Federation of America and a popular writer and speaker on the topics of abortion, ethics, and sexuality. She is a former volunteer pregnancy counselor, helping women and couples decide what they will do about pregnancy. Her writings on the spiritual aspects of unintended pregnancy have appeared in magazines and newspapers nationwide.

Runkle earned her B.A. in Broadcast Communication Arts at San Francisco State University and her Masters of Public Policy at the University of California, Berkeley.

In
Good
Conscience

Introduction: About This Book

I think the lesson is to look inside your own heart and inside yourself for the answer about what's going on, and if you listen to people outside of yourself you can hear ten different stories. I had so many people influencing me, or trying to.

—LENA

Few women talk about their abortion experience, but nearly half of all women under age forty-five in this country will have an abortion at some time. Many more will consider abortion but decide against it. Unfortunately, the silence we keep about our personal abortion experiences deprives other women considering abortion of our knowledge and support—at a time that can be among the most painful and frightening in a woman's life.

The whole thing, pregnancy, is a very isolating experience. You'd think nobody else ever gets pregnant. If men had abortions you couldn't go anywhere without hearing about it, but because women do it it's shut away in the closet somewhere.

—LENA

ABORTION: RIGHT OR WRONG?

When the media talk about abortion, they almost always make it a black-and-white issue. Either you're for or against it. Either it's right or wrong.

This kind of person is pro-choice, that kind is anti-abortion. In reality, of course, things are not that simple.

If you are like most people, you have mixed feelings about abortion. Even people who are strongly pro-choice disapprove of *some* abortions— for example, in the case of a couple who learns at five months that the fetus is female and abort to try for a male. Likewise, some anti-abortion picketers will suddenly become pro-choice when someone in their own family becomes accidentally pregnant. But because we *think* everybody out there feels only one way or the other, many of us are afraid to speak our truth.

It's a fact that many people have very strong feelings about abortion, and some of them have been very unkind to the people who choose it. We've heard of women being judged because they had an abortion, or because they had several, or because they didn't have one and should have. We've also heard them being judged for becoming single mothers, or teen mothers, or getting married because of a pregnancy, or placing a child for adoption, or not using birth control, or just plain having sex, or *not* having sex. Think for a moment about all the negative things you've heard said about women who made those choices. There seems to be no way to win!

It's no wonder that women keep these experiences a secret. Even when we can escape other people's judgment, we judge ourselves. Somehow, no matter what we decide, we fear the choice we make will make us bad people.

The only thing I didn't like was the doctor saying "let's not let this happen again." I felt like, of course not, I didn't do this on purpose.

—Ingrid

WHO SHOULD READ THIS BOOK?

If you have discovered you are pregnant and think you might want to have an abortion, this book is for you. With an unintended pregnancy, your emotions may be going up and down between wild fear and intense excitement—or maybe anger, sorrow, joy, or anxiety. Your mind may be racing between your two basic options: Should you continue the pregnancy or end it? You might change your mind every hour, or tentatively make your decision and then be haunted by doubts. In many ways, the intense pressure of an unintended pregnancy is the worst thing for the decision process. The strong emotions, anxiety, and urgency can make it hard to think clearly, or to know what feels right.

> *I went to the doctor and he said to come back when I'd made up my mind. I told him that's what I was trying to do, but it seemed like there was no one to help me.*
>
> —LISA

What makes the pressure even worse is that you only have a limited time to make your decision—it could be a matter of weeks or even days before it's too late for an abortion. It's one of the most important decisions you'll make in your life, and whether you end up choosing abortion or childbirth you cannot change the choice.

Where Are You Right Now?

Imagine that the line below contains all the ways you could feel about the best choice for you. Where are you today? Put an X on that point on the line.

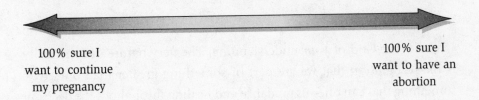

100% sure I
want to continue
my pregnancy

100% sure I
want to have an
abortion

USING THIS BOOK

Deciding whether to have an abortion does not have to be a time of terror or desperation. This book is designed to walk you through the decision process, help calm your mind, and break a decision that may seem over-whelming into small steps that you can take one at a time.

In this book you'll find the facts you need to make an informed deci-sion about your pregnancy, including medical, historical, and legal facts, descriptions of what it's like to have an abortion, suggestions for finding people to support you, and, if you decide to have an abortion, a step-by-step guide to making an appointment. If you decide to continue your pregnan-cy, it will also help you take beginning steps to prepare for parenting or adoption (though it is only a beginning—in these cases you will need resources other than this book).

Most importantly, this book contains write-in sections where you can explore your own feelings, thoughts, and beliefs about abortion. Taking the time to work through these sections could be the most loving thing you can do for yourself at this time. These sections address the emotion-al and spiritual aspects of your decision—not with answers but with *questions*. It may seem that writing short answers to such important questions can't possibly be helpful, but if you'll take the time to write them your answers may surprise you. Getting your answers on paper is like making a map of your own conscience. This map can reveal the inner wisdom that is already part of you. And the writing process itself can be a form of prayer, asking for guidance from a Power greater than yourself, so that you will come to know in your heart what is the right decision.

Does This Mean God?

Yes—the God of *your* understanding. The very nature of spirituality is the recognition that we are part of something greater than ourselves, something that can offer us guidance and healing throughout the decision process. Some people refer to this something as God, but many people have a somewhat different conception and call this guiding force a Higher Power, Goddess, Life Force, the Universe, Great Spirit, or Creator, or they understand the source of spirituality to be nature itself. No one word rings true for everyone, but it is the concept, not the word, that is important. In an effort to use the most neutral and meaningful word, I use the term Higher Power. As you read, you can substitute in your mind the word that works for you.

Does This Book Push Any One Decision?

Absolutely not! This book is pro-choice, which means it supports you no matter what you decide. It can be hard during an unintended pregnancy to find people who truly support you whether you choose abortion, adoption, or parenting. However, *this book will support you.*

There will always be people in the world who want to push women to have babies when they don't feel they can, and still others who will push women to have an abortion when that does not feel right. It is my belief that both kinds of pressure are morally wrong. Your decision about your pregnancy will affect you many times more than it will affect those who may pressure you. You can listen to their opinions, but ultimately it is you who must decide what is best. This is a great freedom, but it is also a great responsibility.

There's this myth that abortion is such an easy decision for everyone. It is for some. Since this was a hard decision for me, I thought I wasn't like the women who choose abortion. I thought I better not have one.

—LISA

Do You Need Other Sources of Help?

This book is no substitute for professional counseling, nor for the love and support of people who care about you (and these are very good to have!). No matter how much support you have, however, it can be difficult to get information—especially when you have only a short time to make a decision. This book provides more information than you can get in a clinic appointment or a few counseling sessions. But medical and mental health professionals can help you address specific issues that are not included in this book.

Good for You

The fact that you are reading this book is a wonderful sign of your self-respect, love, and personal responsibility. Whether you choose to use all or just part of this book—and whether you decide on abortion, adoption, or raising a baby—it is my hope that you will feel right about that decision for the rest of your life.

Exercise: Giving up Judgment

A lot of the stress we face during unintended pregnancy has to do with judgment—we're afraid other people will disapprove of the decision we make, or the fact that we are having sex, or the relationship we're in, and so on. The worst accusations about us might even come from ourselves.

Judging people is a symptom of our unhappiness. When we don't feel good about ourselves we can get into judging other people, which in turn gets us into judging ourselves, which makes us even more unhappy. The only possible solution is to give up this type of judgment entirely. The sooner you stop doing it to yourself and others, the sooner other people's judgments will stop affecting you.

This week, try to catch yourself when you're having a judgmental thought about anyone, including yourself. When it happens, let the judgment go and tell yourself that the person you are judging may be fearful—but is only good.

THE NUMBERS: WHO HAS ABORTIONS?

There is no stereotype of the kind of woman who has an abortion. She is usually someone who has become pregnant by accident, and accidental pregnancy is very, very common. Remember, almost half of all pregnancies are accidents. Many women in this situation decide to continue their pregnancies, but almost half decide that abortion is the best choice for them. In all, about 20 percent of all pregnancies in this country—or 1.5 million a year—result in abortion.

In some rare cases, women with planned, wanted pregnancies end up choosing abortion either because their life circumstances have changed or because doctors discover severe abnormalities in the pregnancy.

DO RELIGIOUS PEOPLE OPPOSE ABORTION?

The majority of religious people in this country support a woman's right to choose abortion, and many of them have had abortions themselves. Most religious groups support abortion too (see Chapter Five). Some religions have an anti-abortion position, but that doesn't mean that all the people in those churches agree with their religious leaders. Even women who believe abortion is wrong sometimes choose abortion for themselves.

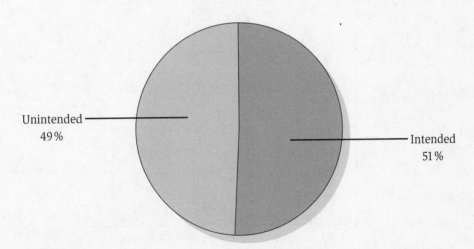

Percentage of Intended and Unintended U.S. Pregnancies. *Source: Alan Guttmacher Institute, 1998*

Note: Unintended pregnancies include those that are not wanted, not planned, or have come at a bad time.

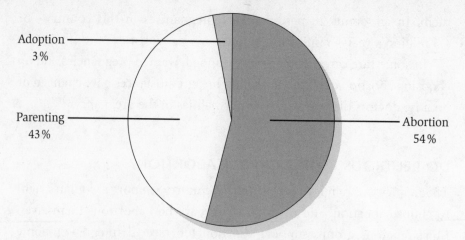

Unintended Pregnancy: What Women Choose. *Source: Alan Guttmacher Institute, 1998; Independent Adoption Center*

Note: This chart does not include pregnancies that end in miscarriage.

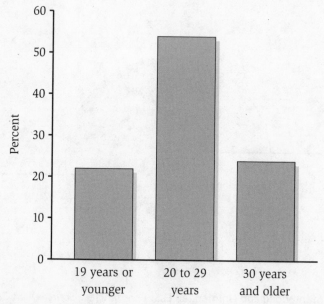

Women Who Choose Abortion: How Old Are They? *Source: Alan Guttmacher Institute, 1998*

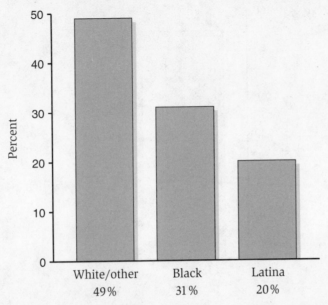

Ethnicity of Women Who Choose Abortion. *Source: Henshaw and Kost, 1996*

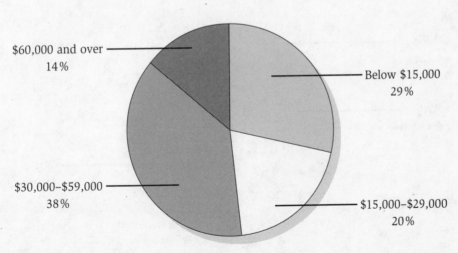

Household Income of Women Who Choose Abortion. *Source: Alan Guttmacher Institute, 1998*

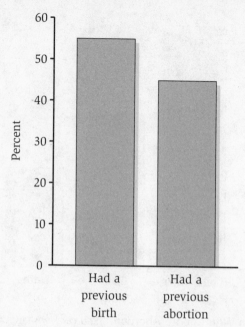

Previous Births and Abortions by Women Who Choose Abortion. *Source: Henshaw and Kost, 1996*

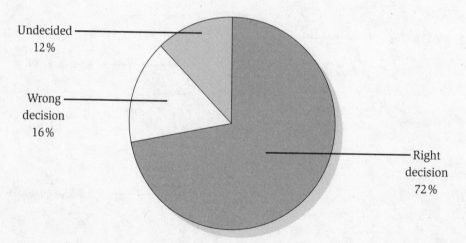

How Women Who Choose Abortion Feel About the Decision Two Years Later.
Source: Major, 1997

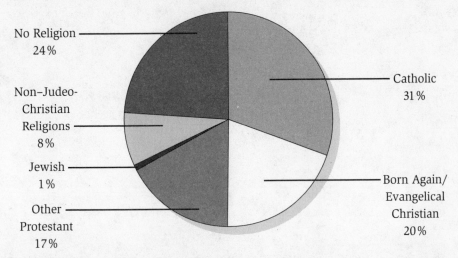

No Religion
24%

Non–Judeo-
Christian
Religions
8%

Jewish
1%

Other
Protestant
17%

Catholic
31%

Born Again/
Evangelical
Christian
20%

Religion of Women Who Choose Abortion. *Sources: Alan Guttmacher Institute, 1998; Henshaw and Kost, 1996*

What to Do as Soon as You Learn You Are Pregnant

I felt angry at my body, like "don't you know I don't want to be preg-nant?" I felt like someone had done this to me, that I was a pawn, that I was going along and suddenly this *happens. I felt like I wasn't in control of my life.*

—LENA

Whether you decide to have an abortion or to continue the preg-nancy, there are some actions you need to take right away. Please read through this chapter carefully to make sure you take the steps neces-sary now, no matter what your decision may be.

CALCULATE YOUR LMP

Whatever you decide to do about your pregnancy, you will need to know the first day of your last menstrual period, or LMP. This is the "start date" of your pregnancy, even though conception probably occurred sometime after this period. This date is used to predict your due date, or when and how an abortion may be performed. If you are not sure, then figure out the range of time within which your last period began—for example, "sometime in March" or "after December 15 when school got out but before Christmas."

If your last period was unusual, especially if it was light and came at an odd time, be sure to note this and be sure to tell your doctor or the clinic staff when discussing your LMP. An unusual period could mean you were pregnant *before* your last period. This is critical information when considering an abortion. When you visit a doctor or clinic, staff can use ultrasound imaging to determine just how far along your pregnancy is.

If there is any chance that you will continue your pregnancy, you should begin prenatal care—a regular program of medical care during your pregnancy—within ten weeks of your LMP.

Elective abortion (that which is not medically necessary) is accessible up until about twenty-six weeks (or six months). If you choose abortion, however, it is much better physically, financially, and (many people feel) ethically to have it within the first twelve weeks. Later abortions are hard to obtain in some areas, as well.

When you call a clinic or doctor, they will always ask for your LMP, so memorize it!

> *At the instant of conception I knew it. I was talking to this being and trying to get it to leave, but it wouldn't go.*
>
> —LENA

TAKE CARE OF YOUR BODY

If there is *any chance* you will continue your pregnancy, taking care of your body is very, very important. Even if you are pretty sure you will end your pregnancy, taking care of your body is still worthwhile, helping you feel better physically, mentally, and spiritually.

Food

Early pregnancy may cause you to eat more or less than usual, to crave certain foods, and even to be disgusted by foods you usually love.

Obey your body's signals—that is, don't force yourself to eat something that turns your stomach, but be sure to eat a variety of nutritious foods when you do eat. Prenatal vitamins can help make sure you get all the nutrients you need. These are available without a prescription at drug stores and clinics.

It was interesting being pregnant. I'm glad I know what it's like, that spacey, strange feeling.

—INGRID

Rest and Exercise

Most women in early pregnancy feel less energetic than usual. As often as possible, obey your body when it tells you it's tired and lie down. Many women find they need an afternoon nap through the first three or four months of pregnancy. Exercise can help keep your energy level up, and is essential to a healthy pregnancy. Exercise should be moderate—long walks, swimming, bicycling, gentle aerobics. Physically intense activities such as football, slam dancing, or some types of weight training can endanger your pregnancy and your own safety. Keep your exercise gentle until you can speak with a doctor about what is safe for you, even if you don't plan to continue your pregnancy.

Drugs and Alcohol

Right now it is best to stop all use of alcohol, tobacco, and other drugs, even those sold over the counter. Use of these substances can lead to serious and even fatal birth defects, even if they are used in only small amounts. If addiction makes it difficult to stop, now is the time to get help. See a doctor as soon as possible, and don't be embarrassed to admit using these substances. Be totally honest so your doctor can get you appropriate help. Most counties have free treatment programs for low-income pregnant women who are drug and alcohol addicted. Some free resources for everyone are Alcoholics Anonymous and Narcotics Anonymous, which are twelve-step programs open to anyone with a desire to stop drinking and using drugs. Meetings are held in cities throughout the country and can be very effective for those who really want to recover. There are also twelve-step programs for eating disorders, nicotine addiction, sex and love addiction, marijuana addiction, and more, so take advantage of any that you would find helpful.

You should also restrict your caffeine intake—it's less harmful than other drugs but if you use too much it can cause problems. Avoid coffee, Coke, Pepsi, Mountain Dew, Dr. Pepper, and caffeinated tea.

If you have concerns about exposure to drugs, alcohol, or other toxic substances during your early pregnancy call your doctor or clinic.

How to Deal with Morning Sickness

Morning sickness is never pleasant, but it feels worse when the pregnancy is not wanted. It usually starts around five or six weeks after the first day of your last menstrual period, gets worse until eight or nine weeks, and tapers off after thirteen weeks. It's called morning sickness because for many women it's worse when they first wake up, but others have it at other times during the day. Some women get it worse than others, and some don't have it at all. The symptoms can range from an occasional queasy feeling to frequent vomiting, triggered by certain food smells, an empty stomach, or nothing at all.

The best way to prevent sickness is to keep something in your stomach at all times, which means having a healthy snack like nuts or fruit to nibble on throughout the day. Some women find that keeping saltine crackers next to the bed is helpful. They can be eaten in the middle of the night and in the morning, a few minutes before getting out of bed. Herbal teas such as chamomile and peppermint can help settle your stomach as well. Avoid fried foods and junk foods, as these can be a sure way to make morning sickness worse.

*I knew right away. I knew because of my breasts. If you're tuned to
your body you know you're pregnant.*

—NAOMI

DON'T WAIT FOR A MISCARRIAGE

One out of six pregnancies ends in what doctors call "spontaneous abortion," commonly called miscarriage. Unfortunately, many women who have second-trimester abortions were those who were "hoping" for a miscarriage. A miscarriage will not save you from pain or having to deal with your pregnancy. Just the opposite—a miscarriage can lead to serious bleeding, infection, and even death. It requires immediate medical attention. And in emergency situations, it can be harder to keep your pregnancy a secret than with a scheduled abortion in a clinic. Remember, the longer your pregnancy continues the more risky your abortion will be—and the more it will cost.

*It was an inconvenience and an intruder. I had the sense that this
spirit was an intruder.*

—LENA

DO NOT ATTEMPT TO GIVE YOURSELF AN ABORTION

Any abortion that is not performed in a licensed clinical setting is potentially very harmful. Unsafe methods include herbal preparations, going on a bumpy ride, drinking a large quantity of alcohol, inserting things into the cervix, getting punched in the stomach, and using toxic douches. These methods are seldom effective in ending a pregnancy, but very effective in causing birth defects, infection, and serious injury and illness to you. All of these complications are likely to put you in the hospital, which is far more expensive and less private than safe, clinical abortion performed by a licensed professional.

Safe, confidential abortion is available to you. If you have concerns about money, privacy, or legal problems, talk to an abortion provider. They will help you!

CALL AN ABORTION PROVIDER

Once you know your LMP, get on the phone and find out where you can have an abortion procedure, even if you probably won't end up having an abortion (see "How to Find a Provider" in Chapter Seven). This is an incredibly important step; it will help you connect now to resources and information that you will absolutely need if you end up choosing abortion. Don't worry that you are making a commitment to any one decision. You're just keeping your options open.

If you are worried about confidentiality, tell the abortion provider. It will give you tips on how to keep your pregnancy and your decision process a secret. It will even work with you to invent a code name so that if you want the clinic to contact you, the caller can say it's "Janie" or "Rosalie" calling, or whatever name you want.

Tell the receptionist that you're considering an abortion and give her your LMP. Tell her especially if you had an unusual period last time, in case you've been pregnant since before your last period. Ask her how long you have until your second trimester begins, and when will be the last day you could get a first trimester abortion at her clinic (if you are in your second trimester, you need to make a decision and an appointment as quickly as possible). Make an appointment within the time frame she gives you, just so you have it. If you end up not needing it—or changing it to an earlier day or needing to postpone it—fine. As a courtesy, you should call twenty-four hours in advance when you need to cancel appointments.

Now that you have an abortion appointment, ask the receptionist if there are any restrictive laws for which you will have to be prepared (see "Laws Restricting Abortion" in Chapter Seven). She can tell you the steps you need to take now so that earlier abortion is an option for you. She can also answer any questions you have.

GET INSURANCE, SECURE AUTHORIZATION, OR FIND ALTERNATIVE FUNDING

Whether you choose to end your pregnancy or continue it, you will need medical care. Now is the time to figure out how you will pay for either option whether you have private insurance, Medicaid, or no insurance at all. For information on ways to pay for abortion or for a continuing pregnancy, see Chapter Seven.

What Happens During an Abortion

It was a harrowing experience, just horrifying, but I never had a moment's doubt that what I was doing was right.

—LENA

The abortion wasn't as bad as I thought it was going to be at all. It was not much worse than having a pap smear done. It wasn't any worse than that.

—SANDRA

With all the hype about abortion, a lot of people are not clear about what actually happens. Technically, an abortion is the deliberate termination of a pregnancy through removal of the embryo or fetus. It is possible to terminate a pregnancy at any time from conception to birth, but 88 percent of abortions are performed in the first trimester.

Most second-trimester abortions are performed before twenty weeks. Less than one-half of 1 percent of abortions are performed after that point. In the third trimester—or, more specifically, after about twenty-six weeks—abortion is only legal in cases where the woman's health is seriously endangered or in cases of severe fetal deformity.

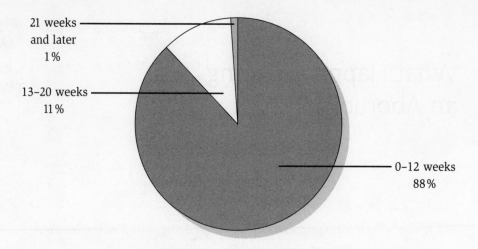

21 weeks
and later
1%

13–20 weeks
11%

0–12 weeks
88%

When Abortions Are Performed. *Source: Russo and Horn, 1995*

A TYPICAL FIRST-TRIMESTER ABORTION

A woman having an abortion will usually begin her visit to the clinic by checking in at the front desk, where she'll receive medical history forms to fill out and handle financial or insurance arrangements. After a while she will be called into the clinic for a urine test to make sure she is really pregnant and a blood test to check whether she is anemic and to determine her blood type. A clinic worker will also check her vital signs—pulse, blood pressure, and temperature.

Before the procedure, a staff member will speak privately with the woman about any questions or concerns she may have about the procedure and provide detailed information about what will happen during the abortion and how it will feel. Most clinics offer counseling, individually or in groups, so that all patients have a chance to talk about the feelings they are experiencing. If a woman is very upset and seems unsure about her abortion decision, clinic staff will suggest she postpone her appointment until she feels more clear.

Most abortion visits involve a lot of waiting. Although the procedure itself takes only a few minutes, the entire visit may take several hours. Many women bring something to read, and most bring a friend, partner, or parent to keep them company. Most clinics will allow this support person to accompany a woman during the abortion itself.

When it's time for the abortion, a clinic worker brings the woman to the exam room and asks her to undress from the waist down. The woman lies on the exam table and puts her feet in stirrups. Many clinics use ultrasound or a sonogram to determine exactly how far along the pregnancy is. A clinic worker presses an imaging device, along with some conductive gel, on the lower part of the woman's stomach. Sometimes the device is inserted in the woman's vagina. The device produces a black-and-white image on a monitor that allows the clinician to see the embryonic sac, the embryo, and the placenta (see next page). If the woman wishes, she can see the image too.

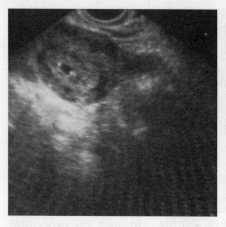

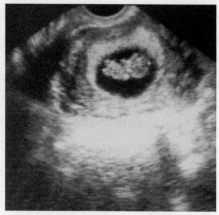

Ultrasound Image of a Five-Week Pregnancy

Ultrasound Image of a Ten-Week Pregnancy

Soon the doctor enters, introduces himself or herself, and begins a vacuum aspiration procedure. First he inserts a *speculum* in the woman's vagina so that her cervix is accessible and visible. (A speculum and other instruments used during the abortion are shown on pages 26–27.) He washes the vaginal area with antiseptic to prevent infection, then injects the cervix with a drug that numbs the area. Some women say they can't feel this injection; others feel a sharp pinch or burning sensation. Another sharp pinch may be felt when the doctor uses a *tenaculum* to hold the cervix steady while he works.

If the abortion is somewhere between the eighth and twelfth week, the doctor may use *dilators* to slowly widen the opening in the cervix. He'll gently insert a narrow rod, then a wider one, until it is wide enough to insert the tip of the *cannula* through the cervix and into the uterus. For many women, having anything inserted through the cervix causes cramping and even a dizzy sensation.

The cannula is attached to a hose that leads to the *aspirator,* a machine that gently suctions out the blood and tissue inside the uterus. Because the embryo is very tiny during the first trimester, the entire pregnancy can be removed through the thin cannula in just a few minutes.

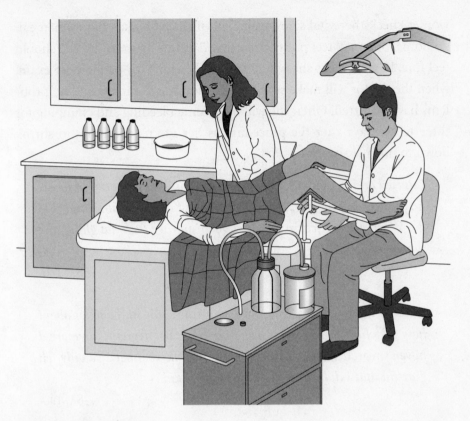

Scene During an Abortion.

(You'll find illustrations of the embryo at various stages of development in Appendix Three.)

As the uterus is emptied, it contracts to its nonpregnant size. This part of the abortion can cause strong cramps, but soon the pain is over. If her blood type is Rh-negative, the woman will have an injection of RhoGAM®. She may also receive a birth control method, such as birth control pills or an injection of Depo-Provera® at this point in her visit.

After a few minutes of rest the woman sits up, puts on a sanitary napkin to catch any blood that may still flow, and dresses. She moves to the recovery room where she can sit in a comfortable chair with a heating pad on her stomach, soothing the cramps. After half an hour or so, a clinic worker checks her vital signs again, and if they are okay the woman can go home. She may feel pretty tired that day, but by morning she should feel fine. In two weeks she will return to the clinic for a follow-up exam, when the doctor will make sure the abortion was complete and no problems have occurred. Often she will have some bleeding and cramping for three to six days after the procedure as her uterus continues to shrink down to normal size.

> *I started crying right after the abortion because it had been so stressful facing all of the people and being honest about what I decided to do. When I left I felt so free and good and we were laughing and making jokes.*
>
> —SANDRA

> *I was on welfare at the time and I wrote the clinic staff a letter about how grateful I was for their help and to not be pregnant anymore. I haven't regretted it since. Every time I think about it I've only felt grateful that I didn't have to have another kid.*
>
> —SANDRA

> *I dealt with it. I grieved. I had no choice. I'm a survivor.*
>
> —NAOMI

ABORTION TERMS

Speculum—a plastic or metal tool inserted in the vagina, then opened to hold vaginal walls apart for the doctor to see and work with the cervix

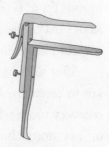

Tenaculum—a tonglike instrument that clamps onto the edge of the cervix and holds it steady during the abortion procedure

Dilators—thin rods that range from the width of a pencil to the width of a man's thumb, used to gradually open the cervix wide enough for the cannula to be inserted

Cannula—a thin plastic tube, attached to an aspirator, that is inserted through the cervix and used to suction out the pregnancy

Laminaria—sticks of seaweed the size of wooden matches, used in second-trimester (and some first-trimester) abortions to dilate the cervix. They are inserted the day before the abortion, sometimes several at a time. They slowly absorb moisture and expand, stretching the cervical opening over a period of several hours.

Curette—a sharp tool used in abortions (usually in the second trimester) to help loosen tissue from the inside of the uterus

Aspirator—an electric machine like a vacuum that collects the contents of the uterus

RhoGAM®—a drug administered to the 10 percent of women who have Rh-negative blood. When an Rh-negative woman is pregnant with an Rh-positive fetus, she can develop antibodies that would cause serious problems for future pregnancies. To avoid these problems, Rh-negative women need an injection of RhoGAM® after abortion or childbirth.

METHODS OF ABORTION

There are two basic kinds of abortion, surgical and medical.

Surgical Abortion

Several types of surgical abortion are available:

Vacuum Aspiration. This is the basic dilation-and-suction method described earlier as a typical first-trimester abortion. It can be used from seven to twelve weeks since the first day of your last period (LMP). Sometimes this technique also involves the use of a *curette* in a process called "dilation and curettage."

Manual Aspiration. This is a very early abortion technique becoming more and more available. It can be used at any time in the first trimester, but is most common between four and six weeks after LMP. Because the pregnancy is so small, the cannula can be very slender and

The Pelvic Area and Tools Used During Abortion.

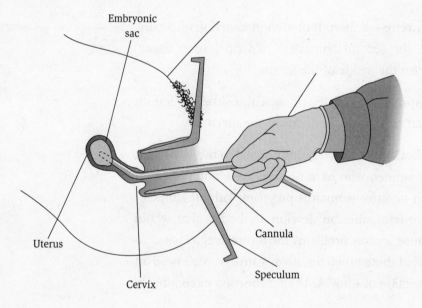

Embryonic sac

Uterus

Cannula

Cervix

Speculum

very little dilation is needed. Instead of an electric aspirator, a syringe is used.

Dilation and Evacuation (D and E). This is used in the second trimester, when the fetus has grown a little larger. The doctor uses instruments together with vacuum aspiration to empty the uterus. The cervix must be dilated more than in the first trimester. Often the doctor will use *laminaria* instead of dilators.

Induction or Instillation. For some very late abortions (which are rare), the doctor injects a drug such as Digoxen through the woman's abdomen and into the sac containing the fetus, which stops the fetal heartbeat. A second drug is administered that causes labor to begin, and the fetus is delivered in a way similar to childbirth.

Medical Abortion

Almost everyone has heard of the "abortion pill"—mifepristone or RU-486. After a lot of legal hassles and media hype, two methods of non-surgical (medical) abortion have finally become available at some U.S. clinics. They are both used as early as when pregnancy is detected and as late as the ninth week of pregnancy, though they are less effective at ending pregnancy beyond the seventh week after LMP. They are just as safe as first-trimester surgical abortions and cost about the same.

Mifepristone (RU-486). This is a pill that blocks the hormone progesterone, causing the lining of the uterus to break down and begin to expel blood from the cervix. A couple of days later, a drug called Misoprostol, a pill or vaginal suppository containing the hormone prostaglandin, is used to start contractions. Misoprostol can have temporary side effects including nausea and vomiting. The pregnancy is usually expelled within twenty-four hours, but it can take several weeks. If nothing happens, the woman is sometimes given an extra dose of

Misoprostol. Less than 5 percent of the time such women end up needing surgical abortion, which is not covered in the original price of the abortion. Another downside of this method is that the woman must make two to four trips to the clinic instead of one or two as required for first-trimester surgical abortions. Finally, the fact that no one can predict when the pregnancy will be expelled means it could happen when the woman is not at home or does not have support. Early in the pregnancy the embryo is so tiny it can seldom be recognized, but this could still be upsetting for some women. Many clinics offer counseling to support women through this experience.

Women who choose this method say they prefer it to surgical abortion because it doesn't involve instruments entering or "invading" the body. Some women feel physically, emotionally, or even morally uncomfortable with the idea of an invasive procedure.

Methotrexate. This drug is somewhat similar to Mifepristone but is given by injection. It is followed five to seven days later by Misoprostol to cause contractions and expulsion of the pregnancy, but again this sometimes takes weeks. About one in ten women using this method ends up needing surgical abortion.

Which method of abortion is best for a given pregnancy often has to do with how far the pregnancy has advanced.

HOW SAFE IS ABORTION?

First-trimester abortion is one of the safest surgical procedures. It is seven times safer than childbirth and twice as safe as a shot of penicillin. The risk of heavy bleeding, cramping, or infection is less than one in a hundred, and these problems can almost always be solved fairly simply. The longer the pregnancy has continued, the higher the risks from abortion, though even later in pregnancy abortion remains safer than childbirth.

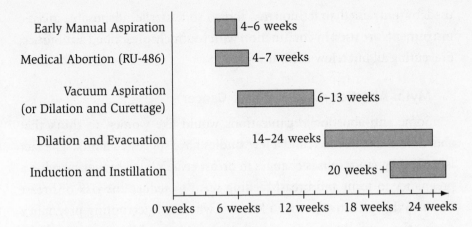

Early Manual Aspiration	4–6 weeks		
Medical Abortion (RU-486)	4–7 weeks		
Vacuum Aspiration (or Dilation and Curettage)	6–13 weeks		
Dilation and Evacuation	14–24 weeks		
Induction and Instillation	20 weeks +		

0 weeks   6 weeks   12 weeks   18 weeks   24 weeks

Abortion Methods: When They Can Be Used.

In about one in five hundred abortions the uterus is perforated—that is, a tear occurs from the use of abortion instruments—but these usually do not need to be repaired. In extremely rare cases women having an abortion will end up needing a hysterectomy—complete removal of the uterus. The risk of death from abortion is one in two hundred thousand, meaning that about seven or eight of the 1.5 million women per year who have an abortion in the United States die as a result.

The single most important thing you can do to reduce the risk of problems is to have the abortion early in the pregnancy, when risks are lowest (Russo and Horn, 1995).

MYTHS ABOUT ABORTION

Although abortion does have some risks, a lot of women have heard that it is much more dangerous than it really is. Here are some of the most common myths about abortion.

Myth: Abortion Makes You Sterile

This myth is left over from the bad old days when abortion was illegal and when unclean, inappropriate instruments such as coat hangers were used by untrained practitioners. Today, soft, sterile, disposable plastic instruments are used in conjunction with routinely prescribed antibiotics, preventing all but a few complications.

Myth: Abortion Causes Breast Cancer

Some anti-abortion organizations would like women to think that abortion leads to cancer, and a few studies have suggested a link. The fact is, early pregnancy causes changes in breast cells. We know that carrying a pregnancy to term and breast-feeding seem to reduce the risk of breast cancer. What scientists want to know is whether interrupting pregnancy during those cell changes worsens the risk of cancer. Most research on the subject has *not* shown a cancer connection. Organizations such as the American Medical Association and the American Cancer Society say more study will be needed, but so far no link can be proved.

> *At this point in time I feel okay with it all, like it was something that was supposed to happen and it happened and that's it. I don't feel guilt or blame, or like I did anything wrong.*

> —LENA

Myth: Abortion Causes Permanent Psychological Damage

Again, anti-abortion organizations have tried to excite the media and scare women about a phenomenon called "postabortion syndrome." No such problem is recognized by the American Medical Association, the American Psychological Association, or other professional organizations. In reality, the most common emotion women experience after an abortion is relief. Over time, women who have abortions do not have higher rates of depression than comparable women who never have an abortion or than those who carry an unintended pregnancy to term (Major, 1997). About one in five, however, says she would not have chosen abortion if she had the decision to make again.

In Good Conscience

About 2 percent experience more serious depression; these women tend to be those who were very unsure about their abortion decision in the first place and may have been under pressure from someone close to them to go through with it. This should never happen! Abortion providers do everything they possibly can to make sure that the woman freely and clearly chooses abortion without pressure from others.

Grief and sadness and anger are sometimes part of healing. I can't tell you what it's like to give someone permission to cry when she thinks she's supposed to be holding it back. It's okay to feel betrayed by your body when you tried to prevent this but nothing worked. It's alright to forgive yourself.

—CAROL, ABORTION PROVIDER

I had a suicide attempt three months after my abortion. It was part of those big feelings of self-loathing. I'm certainly not blaming the abortion, but I know if I had talked through the experience with someone I would have been in a safer, better place.

—SARAH

Depression After Abortion: Who Is Affected? Depression and anxiety levels are highest for most women before an abortion, but some women will feel depressed afterward. There is no sure way to know who they will be, but here are some risk factors (Major, 1997):

1. History of mental health problems
2. Low self-esteem
3. Lack of support from friends and family
4. Poor relationship with male partner
5. Inner conflict about the decision
6. High stress levels from other aspects of life

7. Pressure from others to decide one way or the other

8. Exposure to anti-abortion picketing

WHAT DOES ABORTION COST?

For those whose insurance doesn't cover the procedure, first-trimester abortions cost about $250–$350 in clinics, but can cost more in hospitals and doctors' offices. The cost goes up approximately $100 a week to as high as $2,500 or more for a second-trimester abortion. For information on paying for an abortion, see Chapter Seven.

My abortion was physically painful. My body doesn't react well to being invaded—it's incest stuff. I really think it was emotional pain being put on the physical level because I didn't know where else to put it.

—LISA

I chose not to use any anesthesia. I was punishing myself for getting pregnant. In truth it was the mental pain and not the physical that hurt. I just dealt with it, thinking "well, that's what you get." That's how I've been about pain all my life.

—NAOMI

I've heard stories of women who were put to sleep for abortions who never got to connect with the loss part because they were asleep and when they woke up they simply weren't pregnant anymore. In my experience women get a lot more from some empathy and support than they ever did from ten milligrams of Valium. People have pain when they don't have drugs, but I don't know that pain is always a bad thing. Valium is like drinking in that it numbs you. For women with issues about control or sexual abuse, that loss of control can do

In Good Conscience

*more harm than good. Breathing and focus can replace drugs much
more successfully.*

—CAROL, ABORTION PROVIDER

ANESTHESIA: DO I NEED DRUGS FOR PAIN?

Almost all abortions include local anesthetic—an injection in the cervix
to dull some of the pain of dilation. Some clinics also offer various levels
of pain medication, including Ibuprofen tablets or stronger, narcotic
drugs such as Diprovan. Some clinics and hospitals also offer the option
of general anesthesia (when you're asleep) or "twilight sleep" (a light
sleep), though these often cost extra.

Although women's pain levels vary, first-trimester abortions are
almost always bearable without narcotic pain relief; it is really a matter of
choice. Later abortions tend to require stronger pain relief. You can discuss this with your provider.

DOES THE EMBRYO OR FETUS FEEL PAIN?

Early in the pregnancy, the fetus lacks the kind of nerve connections
between body and brain that would be necessary to have any feeling at all.
At about twenty-one to twenty-three weeks, these connections are beginning to form. By thirty-two weeks, the fetus has brain waves similar to that
of a newborn, and probably has a similar capacity to feel pain (Russo and
Horn, 1995).

How It Feels:
Eight Women Share Their Stories

SHARON, 29

On a spiritual level, deciding to have an abortion was very difficult. There were times when I felt clear, and other times when I felt maybe I was doing something wrong. My boyfriend and I are thinking about marriage, but we're really focused on our goals right now. We have these shitty jobs as a house cleaner and a tow-truck driver, but I'm training to be a nurse, and he's training to be a firefighter. We've worked for these goals too hard to lose it right now. Still, I thought maybe God was saying this is the time and I'm choosing the time for you. We had to ask ourselves—is it time?

I had dreams about pregnancy the whole time I was pregnant, even before I knew I was pregnant. There were babies all around me, which made it even more difficult. I ran into a neighbor who was a month and a half pregnant and she started talking about it and saying how sick she felt—and I'm keeping this all inside because I didn't want the whole world to know that I was pregnant. It happened again with another neighbor. She was asking did I know what it was like to have morning sickness, and I said, "No, I hear it's really nasty." I almost had to deny what I was going through to protect myself from other people. I never knew how they were going to react.

I loved being pregnant. Even though I was sick as a dog and lethargic, I felt beautiful and different from what I normally feel. I think he saw that. He was very attentive and nurturing, 200 percent more than ever before, even though he's that way already. The whole time we both knew that we were going to have an abortion. It wasn't going to be too far. That's what made it even more beautiful. We knew that in the future we were going to have kids and it would be perfect. We'll have our house and we'll have our careers. He had said before the pregnancy, "When you get pregnant, I want the focus to be completely on the pregnancy, not on school and where we're going to get the next dollar." Of course I cried days and nights—it was sad but I think it was more the hormones that threw me off. In the back of my mind I knew that this wasn't the time.

I was using the rhythm method when I got pregnant, you know, the thermometer method. I was using that for five years and never got pregnant. This made it even more confusing for me because I'm finally with the man of my dreams, so I thought maybe this really is meant to be. I had numerous dreams that it was a boy, which made it more difficult, because I really want a boy. I dreamt that I met this woman and she was psychic. She started talking about a boy. She asked, "Did somebody have an abortion that you know of?" And I ended up telling her yes, I just went through an abortion. She said, "Well, it was a boy," and I woke up crying. It was spooky because I felt people on the outside were judging me for my decision and criticizing me.

I had a lot of fear when it came down to the abortion itself. My boyfriend mentioned a lot of nervousness and not wanting to come in the room with me. My mom said, "He really should be in there with you because he helped create it and you made this decision together." I told him I really needed to have him with me. I was going to be put under [general anesthesia] and all this incest stuff came up, and it was going to be a male doctor so it was really important to me that my boyfriend be there. He said he was really scared, and I saw that it wasn't just me in this situation. I had to pay attention to him and let him know I understood. He ended up going in with me.

We didn't tell my boyfriend's parents because his sister-in-law had thirteen abortions. His parents were going on and on about how you can't mess with the spirit that many times. We knew they would support us but it was too hot an issue at the time. I told my family. My mom was more afraid that I would regret my decision and she wanted my boyfriend and me to talk through it. I said we'd talked through it numerous times and we were clear. She really wanted a grandchild and that really added to my fears. My sister's been trying to get pregnant for years and years. She even offered to take the baby, but that was definitely out of the question because she's not stable emotionally or financially. I didn't want anybody else to bring up our child. Plus, I made a decision a long time ago that I would break the cycle of dysfunction, and I plan to do everything I can to make my children's life as different as I can.

I feel completely peaceful about my decision. Right after the abortion I felt relief—you know, I get my life back! There were so many things put on hold until I could get through the abortion and heal from it. I couldn't get the energy to take care of things. I think God is okay with it. When I had a car accident recently it brought me back to the abortion; it made me think I was being punished. I always wonder whether on a spiritual level it was right or wrong—will I have to face it when I die? It's always there. It probably always will be. I have fears I won't be able to have kids and I think—What if that was my only chance? What if something happened to me or my boyfriend and we couldn't have kids? I think the changes I went through were normal and healthy. The only thing that could have made it easier is if I had some spiritual guide come to me and say, "This is what you really need to do."

It won't happen again. We've decided that we're not going to have intercourse until we want to have a child. We still have sex, and it's actually very nice. It's enabling us to reach a lot of different levels of intimacy, and a lot of ways to have sex without having sex. We plan on having sex on our honeymoon. I went out and got a diaphragm, but we decided it would be really different to try to get to our honeymoon without having intercourse. No, there's no date set. We're so strong on not having to have an abortion again that we're willing to put that part of our sex life aside. He jokes around—"You wait till our honeymoon! I'm gonna get you so hard you'll be pregnant the next day."

Still, I don't look back with regret. I feel good about what we did. I don't even regret getting pregnant; that in itself was a gift. I know now what I'm going to have to go through when I'm pregnant. I was given a taste of it, of what that would be like. I got to see how my boyfriend would react with me, and he's going to be the best father. I feel like that was a real gift.

BEATRIZ, 30

I was twenty-four when I found out I was pregnant. I wanted the whole fairy-tale thing, but the guy I was going out with was really abusive and told me to get an abortion. He was having affairs and he didn't want the baby. At first I was happy with this decision but then I was really sad. I cried a lot. It wasn't my Catholic beliefs, it was more my personality. I wasn't ready for it. I went to counseling at the clinic where they did abortions. I started picturing the baby, the way it looked inside and what it would look like when it grew up. I told the counselor I couldn't deal with it. So I went through with the pregnancy.

I went through hell for nine months. I was a basket case. My boyfriend wanted a miscarriage so he threw me against the wall. It was really hard because my mother wanted me to have an abortion too. It was confusing because I was raised in a Catholic family. We're from Mexico, and the discrimination with single moms is pretty bad. She didn't want the traditional Mexican family thing to look bad. I still hold resentment about that. This is her grandson.

I hit rock bottom emotionally. I went to a battered women's shelter for counseling, and a lot of things that I thought were okay I learned were not okay. They made me focus a lot on my personality and me, and once you get that self-esteem up, that changes your choices a lot.

I stayed with my boyfriend for four years. I ended up in a custody battle with him! My son's father always tries to win him over when he has custody. I wish I had just tried to be a single mom from the start. But all those experiences made me pretty strong.

Three years after my son was born I started going to church. I started telling people what I feel about everything. I had friends who went through what I did and I supported them. I think you've got to know what your feelings are. Other people's opinions don't matter. I did hear everyone's opinion, and mostly what I heard was negative. I told them I'm the one who is going to make the decision.

I never realized what it was to be a single mom, and now I know there's so much discrimination about it. People were very bold. They would come up to me and say I just had a baby for money. Or they'd ask, "Weren't you using birth control?" It caused a lot of stress. It still happens. If I'm dressed nice it's okay, but if I'm in jeans it starts again. I don't get welfare but even if I did. . . . I give more support to my child than some of my married friends.

My son is now six years old. I talk with my son about life and tell him what it's about. He changed my life, he made me really different. Every day I see him and say if I hadn't fought through this, this child would be dead. If anyone tries to hurt him I go off! I have a college fund for him now. I used to have a government job and I sold cosmetics on the side, so I saved money. I quit my job and went back to school. Now I'm a medical assistant. I work in a clinic, I want to go into counseling. I applied to the state university.

Now I have a spiritual life. I'm a Baptist now. There's a seminar sometimes, I tell people what I went through, helping women learn to be strong and not depend so much on a man. People say why don't you go against abortion, and I say no, I was so close to doing it that I know what they're going through. I still have unresolved stuff about how people treated me. They say my son is too outspoken, he fights back. I guess he got it from me.

TRISH, 36

I've had two abortions. The first time I was nineteen and I was living with my boyfriend and I had a tubal pregnancy. In this case I had no choice because tubals will kill you. I was in the hospital for a couple of days. Well, I was really careful after that and used a diaphragm religiously. When I was twenty-one I was living with someone again and we were on vacation on the beach and didn't have everything with us. We had sex without spermicide and I was pregnant again. I was waitressing and didn't yet have plans for college. We were serious but young and had no plans for marriage. He came with me for the abortion and insisted on being in the room. He was really sweet and they let him in, which was not the clinic's normal procedure. He held my hand. It was a typical first-trimester vacuum procedure. It wasn't really painful, not like I had been led to believe. There was just some cramping. I was a little nervous, but I think it helped having someone with me.

I didn't feel any guilt. Some women, even those who are very pro-choice, talk about having dilemmas and guilt. I didn't feel anything. No regrets whatever. I don't mean to sound crass, but frankly, it wasn't any more psychologically damaging or soul-searching than a dental extraction. I knew I wasn't ready for motherhood at twenty-one with no husband and no job prospects. It didn't even cross my mind to go through with this pregnancy, even for adoption. I didn't see the point.

Later my mother came over to my apartment and visited. She's Catholic, and I was raised Catholic too. Abortion was something she may not have approved of for herself but she wasn't judgmental. Now that she has no grandchildren maybe she thinks differently. As it happens, tomorrow I'm going in to have my fallopian tubes cleared. I've been trying for two years to get pregnant and hopefully this will work. [Note: Trish's fertility problems are not related to her past abortion.] Do I have tinge of regret about my abortion now? Yes. Fifteen years after my abortion I am faced with the fact that I may never have a biological child and there was a time when I could have. My life could be hell, and I was still drinking heavily and doing drugs back then. But I still think, what if? Is this some kind of divine retribution? I don't know.

SIMONE, 25

I never wanted to have a baby just so I could love him. I had him because when I was eleven in front of the TV, I saw an anti-abortion thing in front of the White House. My friend and I were just appalled, we said how dare they, women have the right to choose! I felt a slap. It was my dad and he slapped me. He said you never kill a child, and he said if you ever get pregnant you will have the child, and that's why at sixteen I made that decision with no hesitation. At that time my parents were doing a lot of drugs, so I had already been out of the house a couple years, staying with friends. I started having sex at fourteen. Where I grew up, kids were having sex in fourth and fifth grade, so I started late. I wasn't a virgin—it was just the first time I consented.

I just blocked the pregnancy out of my mind. Months kept going by. I never got the birds-and-bees talk and didn't know about my body. People would ask was I pregnant and I said no. My boyfriend wanted me to have an abortion. He took me to the clinic and filled out the paperwork and everything. But I made the decision to keep my child. That's my son; he's eight. When I finally received prenatal care I was seven months. My boyfriend's parents didn't find out until the day the baby was released from the hospital. I'm African-American and he was Caucasian and Latino. Because of the biracial thing, they had all this hostility.

During my baby's first year, I was devoted to school and to my son. My teachers encouraged me to go to college. I graduated from high school and got a scholarship. While I was going to school and working, my boyfriend was out exploring other females and started playing head games with me—games that turned into physical abuse. Then he started selling drugs. I didn't want that. I took scholarships and went off to Los Angeles to a junior college. I called him and it was like, "Oh, I love you Simone," so he came down and next thing you know I was pregnant again. That's when I had my first abortion. I was put to sleep. I was devastated when I woke up, because I never thought I would do that, what with my family's values. I was still naïve about birth control. I got pregnant about a year after that, and had another abortion. After that I came back home. I lived with some roommates who were educating me about condoms. I had another new boyfriend by now. We were using condoms and the pill but I was not taking pills faithfully and I got pregnant, and this time I had a daughter. I was twenty, and I decided I couldn't have any more abortions. It wasn't the child's fault, it was me being naïve. But then I got pregnant again and had an abortion. And then I had another one. I had so many abortions and covered them up. I never told anyone. I finally get to tell it now. I had ulcers. I felt awful about the kind of person I was.

I started doing research on how could I help girls in my community who were on their own and help them prevent pregnancy. I was a teenager who used abortion as birth control and educated myself and knew better. It's avoidable. I know when I leave this world I'll have to deal with it, so now I give so much back. I teach kids. I'm teaching them not to need abortion in the first place. Abstaining is good, but for those that choose not to abstain, I tell them how to protect themselves. I talk to those who are already having sex. Some I reverse through talking to them, and tell them it's not too late. But you need that support. It's an emotional need. I was satisfying emotional needs, the need to feel love, the need to be wanted.

I'm going through a court battle for both kids. The men wanted me to have abortions and now they're fighting for my kids. I think, how dare you?—with both of the kids' dads—I had to give up a child because of you and now you're trying to take my child! And who feels the emotional damage from abortion? The first child's father, I made him stay in the room and watch so he could see what I went through. They don't remember that that's the path that only women have to go through.

It always goes back to the abortion. If he would have been like this back then, I could have kept my child. I don't understand why I don't have the right to fight him because he wanted me to have an abortion. Women are punished if we make the decision to have an abortion and we're punished if we choose to have the child. If I try to take any rights away from him they'll snatch the child away from me. If I refuse his requests it's called restraint and they'll snatch her away and give him full custody. The only reason they want these kids is so they don't have to pay child support.

If I could do it again I wish I could have carried the pregnancies to term and placed the kids for adoption. I feel it was selfish and naïve, what I did. At the time I was a child and thought like a child. I made it, but at the same time I lost a lot of things. I had cervical cancer. I have emotional scars. But I'm also abstaining from sex one day at a time, and it's been eight months now. I'm going through a domestic violence program. Every step of the way I've sought help for myself. I'm a Christian. The church has helped me, and I help the church, telling them they can't just tell us not have sex without support. By volunteering and telling my life story I got into health education. I started learning more stuff. I just take the prevention message back to the community, juvenile halls, jails, substance abuse programs, high schools, and elementary schools. I never wanted to be a statistic. I believe that through education and responsibility we have to avoid that. This is a way I can give back.

CLAUDIA, 40

I got pregnant at the age of thirty. I found out I was pregnant about five days after I had a break-in in my house and was attacked in my bed. I had been seeing a nice fellow for a couple of weeks, to have sex with and not really to have a relationship. I didn't tell anyone that I was pregnant because I needed to think for myself.

At the time I was helping to lead a meditation group with a focus on healing. One Wednesday night I went to the center to lead the group and no one showed up. I fell asleep for about an hour. And I woke up and realized it was after 9:00 and time to go home and I locked the center up and went to my car and had the key in my hand when I heard a voice saying, "My name is Rose and I'm your child." My spiritual experience for the last fifteen or twenty years has never included any type of audible sound or voice in my head. I got into the car and sat there and she spoke to me. She said, "I am looking forward to having you be my mother but I want you to know this is your decision and whatever decision you make is perfectly fine with me. If you choose not to continue this pregnancy I will be waiting." I sat in the car and cried for about an hour, feeling very grateful and very sad at the same time. I knew I would not be able to deal with the stress following the break-in and attack and having no money and no real support for having a child in my life.

I proceeded a couple of weeks later to have the abortion. My sister knew about it. And she had told my father without asking my permission. He came up and spent the day with me and for the first time he and I had a real honest discussion about sexuality and birth control and choices that people make. It was his first chance to be supportive of me, to show me that he didn't judge me for my mistake in getting pregnant and to be there for me as one adult for another, and as a father to a daughter. About a month later I participated in a counseling with my ministers. In my practice we channel our higher selves and the message that I received during this counseling was very similar to the reassurance that my child Rose had given me in the car. Ever since then I have felt a full heart relationship with this being named Rose. And although its been ten years, and I'm sad that I'm not yet married and ready to have a child, the relationship has given me great comfort and has been a source of joy for me.

So I went to an abortion clinic, sat in the waiting room, had my name called, interviewed with someone about my choice, and then I was taken into a room where I was given general anesthesia. It was my choice, much preferable to being conscious and hearing and feeling the procedure. When I woke up I wasn't feeling terrific but I felt comfortable enough to go and have lunch with my family. Afterward I went home to nap for an hour or two. When I woke up it was a beautiful day and my father and I sat in the sun and talked. He was there—he met me at the clinic, actually. He and I talked for a couple hours and then we went to dinner and a movie. Actually I can't think of a better way for a day like that to go.

My partner paid for half of the cost of the abortion. We decided not to see each other anymore, simply because we were done. Having something as emotional as a pregnancy happen between us made us realize that we really shouldn't be seeing each other. We were being too casual. We went to the movies together the night he gave me the money. I never felt uncomfortable in his presence after that. It was just time to part. He was supportive. He would not have objected to me bringing the child into the world but he did not choose to be a father so he wouldn't have wanted a role in the child's life.

I do believe that a fetus is life and is alive, that from the moment of conception life exists. But I also believe that souls choose to be born or to live a certain amount of time in the womb and then depart, or they choose to be aborted, because they are on a path to give them certain experiences and I believe that it is the soul that is of paramount importance, not the flesh. Given my agreement with my child, who is eternal, I did nothing other than delay her return to the earth by agreement with her. I deeply desire a child, and I hope it happens. Sometimes I feel in despair of meeting anyone. But I also have a feeling that perhaps I'm not going to give birth to this child. It's possible that she'll come to me in the form of an adoption, and when my life has stabilized financially, I will pursue every avenue to make that happen.

KAREN, 24

My first abortion was at eighteen and it was very hard. I went through a lot with that and I said I would never do it again. I felt really guilty, you know, if I hadn't gotten pregnant this would never have happened. I was so depressed. When I was young, my family picketed an abortion clinic with our church. At that time my parents were totally against abortion. But I was able to talk to my dad about it. We talked at length of my different choices.

My dad's really open. We all became really close when my mom left. I had no one else to tell. My dad doesn't judge us. He's there for us and listens to us and he won't tell us what he thinks we should do. He said, "Write the pros and cons on a piece of paper; any decision you make will be the best decision you could make at the time." It was very helpful. He went with me to the hospital and he was there with me.

The abortion was awful physically. I couldn't stop shaking. Dad was so scared. So was I. It was a bad experience—invading. The first time my dad was in the waiting room. A nurse was with me and talking to me and when I'm nervous I'll talk a lot, and I was trying to take my mind off what they were doing. The most awful part of it is you hear it. I kept singing to myself. I had no counseling. I wish I had some.

Afterward, I was really sad and shocked and I didn't know how to deal with it. My dad and I went and lit a candle when the child would have been one year old. It tears up your body. It's a shock to your system and to your psyche.

I got pregnant two years later with my son and decided to keep him because I didn't want to go through another abortion. When he was a year old I was pregnant again, and I knew I couldn't raise the child, and at the time I wasn't even thinking of going full term, so I chose abortion again. It was another hard time, but you just move out of your body. I just knew that I could get through it. It was the best decision.

Six months later I was pregnant again. I really didn't want another abortion. I didn't want that agony and pain again, but I knew I couldn't raise another child. My son requires a lot of my attention and I couldn't have taken care of an infant and a three-year-old. My boyfriend was not a big part of our lives at that time, and I wasn't working and I did not want to be on welfare for the rest of my life. If I were to have another child then it would have made it harder for me to get my life together. Still, I was not in good space to think about adoption. I knew I couldn't do that. It wasn't me.

I had a change of heart because of listening to a friend who can't have a child, and her difficulties. All these shows were coming on television about adoption—just being able to give someone the gift of life because they are unable to have children of their own. I thought, I am so able to have a child. It's so easy to get pregnant and yet so easy to get rid of it. I was probably three weeks pregnant. The spiritual side of me said it was just meant to be, even though I knew I wasn't going to raise this child.

At three months I called an agency that specializes in open adoptions. Open adoption is great. I chose Mark and Christine to be my baby's parents. They were the first couple I called, I just knew, I had goose bumps. Someone had sent Mark and Christine to me and it was meant to be. Christine and I hit it off and we had so much in common. So I got to know them for six months. At least I knew my decision early, not when I was farther along like some birth mothers. I was able to call her and let her know how I was feeling. During the pregnancy you go through different grieving periods. I'd worked through it so I wouldn't hold any resentment. I got really sad toward the end. It was something that I never ever dreamed that I'd be doing. I knew I could change my mind. But I still felt it was the right thing to do.

During the birth, Christine was my coach. She will never give birth and I wanted her to have that. Kaylie was born and stayed in the room with me the first night. It was very hard. Then the Barnetts came. It was such a chaotic day. It was another one of those body experiences. I just wasn't there. They let me put her in the car seat. Watching them drive away in front of me was so hard. And still I felt like it was the right thing to do. We're still friends. We don't even just call about Kaylie. They have an older adopted child. Christine helps me with my son. Now I'm part of their extended family. They live in Idaho, so I went out there for Kaylie's first birthday. The trip was awesome. Christine didn't feel threatened by me. I didn't feel tense. I could be myself. I saw Kaylie standing in the airport; she had just started walking. I had tears of joy. She looks just like her birth dad.

My boyfriend and I are working things out, so he hears about Kaylie through me. He's dealing with his feelings but its very difficult for him.

He's always wanted a girl; he has two sons already. He hasn't really worked through the grieving process. He'll go to birth-parent support group meetings with me. He says he will never see Kaylie unless she wants that when she gets older. He says he will never be able to look her in the eye. He could change. In the last year he's changed a lot. Because of his irresponsibility he was really hard on himself—just the fact that he couldn't take care of her. If, when I was pregnant with her, he would have been the person he is now, this wouldn't have ever happened.

Spiritually I've gotten stronger, I don't judge people like I used to, when it comes to pregnancy and life experiences. It's given me a total different perspective on life. There's just so much out there, giving the gift of life to Mark and Christine, it's indescribable. That is meaningful for me.

CECILIA, 33

My experience of being pregnant was horrific. I was really nauseous and puking the whole time and I worked in a restaurant and the smell of food just made me sick. I was twenty-two. I was in a relationship with this guy, using birth control, but one time we didn't use it and that's why. I went to a clinic to get the pregnancy test and the counselor wanted to talk to me about my method of birth control and I lied and said I had been using the pill and she just looked at me and said it's really rare that you would get pregnant if you were on the pill but I insisted I was because I was really ashamed. I was ashamed of getting pregnant. I don't remember any discussion about whether we would have an abortion—it just seemed obvious.

My boyfriend came with me. He was in the room when they did it. He saw the fetus and it really flipped him out. What I remember poignantly about the whole experience was I was drugged and I went home, took a nap, and when I woke up he wasn't there. He left a note saying he went to a Hitchcock movie and it was clear that he was fucked up emotionally. He couldn't be there for me and he escaped.

I called my best friend and told her what had happened. She said, "That's crazy, come over, you shouldn't be alone," so I went over and we got rip-roaring drunk. I got really happy when we were drunk and we were toasting my abortion—"Here's to your abortion!" I remember feeling really numb about the whole thing. I didn't really tell anyone except her. Later, my friend's sister came up and expressed this sympathy—my friend had told her. I remember saying, "What? What's this sympathy? What for?" I guess I was really detached from it.

So how did I heal? I don't think I really did. What I had access to was alcohol, and that's what I used that night. That was the beginning of the end of that relationship. I felt completely abandoned. I think I said something to him about it and he was sorry but it was like he just flipped out. We were living together at the time. We lived together a couple more months but I never really trusted him after that.

I don't think I had any concept of God or guilt. A lot of people talk about, "Oh, my unborn baby, I grieved and said goodbye," and I never felt anything like that. I think I was just so clear from this feminist point of view that this baby was not real yet. I don't know if I would feel that now but I did then. Now I might have more feelings about it. I might also have a spiritual experience—I'm deeply spiritual now. I think I was kind of callous about the whole thing but I was also young and a busser at a restaurant and hadn't finished college yet. I can't really imagine what would have happened to me if I had had a kid. Looking back at it now I never doubted it was the right decision and I don't doubt that now, but I guess the thing I regret is I didn't have any way—because I was so sure I was right—I didn't have any way to even admit to any other feelings. I wasn't raised religiously so I didn't have any of that baggage that it's a sin—I never felt any of that. But I also didn't have any way to have a more full experience of it. I treated it like a procedure. I had to go and get a procedure done to my body. It didn't quite seem real.

It certainly made me take birth control seriously. I was a little lax about it until then, but I knew I didn't want to go through it again, the pain. It was physically painful. And the shame that I had—yeah, I did feel shame and I think that's why I didn't tell people that I had had an abortion, that I had been pregnant, and why I lied to the counselor. I had a lot of shame about it, but not guilt or misgivings. Looking back the one thing I really regret, now that I'm sober, is it seems clear that getting drunk was the only thing I knew how to do in response to that, and also getting drunk was the way I could connect with my friends around it, and that's probably what I would have done with my boyfriend if he had stayed around.

If I had it to do over again I would have done some soul-searching about it, and not just made a decision without thinking about it. That's easy to say, though, because I have a spiritual life I didn't have then. That's the reason I had to get drunk—I had no tools to deal with spiritual questions about things like life and death and birth, no way to feel a connection with everyone. Today I do, and I feel a sense of peace and serenity about the past.

ANNIE, 27

I was twenty-one when I found myself pregnant. I discussed it with my partner, but overwhelmingly when I look back I felt it was my decision to make. Even if he had told me to have the baby I still would have followed through with my decision to have an abortion.

An interesting thing happened when I made that decision and when I made the appointment. Even though I had been with Hal for a year, and we had just moved in together, and I cared about him a lot—when this all came about I really didn't want him to go with me. Probably the best decision I could ever have made was to not have him go. It actually put a huge stress on our relationship. He didn't understand it. He felt suspicious and didn't understand why I didn't want him to go. But I knew if I went with Hal I was going to wind up taking care of him or that he was going to think that I needed to be overly taken care of. I needed to be with someone who understood.

My girlfriend who went with me that day had never had an abortion but I just felt like she understood. In the waiting room all these women were with their boyfriends and husbands and everyone was so serious and there was so much tension. I think my girlfriend, as a woman, understood the severity of what was going on and the immensity of the decision I had made, but with that understanding we were able to talk about other things and laugh a little and be comfortable. I had made my decision and I didn't want to sit there and mope about it. I needed to be with someone who understood that.

I was a little disappointed in my experience at the clinic. I've always used this place, so when I decided to have an abortion that was the place that I trusted. I remember feeling like I was on an assembly line. The doctor whooshed in and whooshed out. The procedure was pretty quick, and it hurt a little bit. I felt like I was going to throw up afterward and I told the nurse and she gave me a little tray but I really needed just a few minutes in that room just to calm my stomach and calm myself and I felt like they really just wanted me out of there to get the next person in.

Afterward I went into a recovery area. It was like a room where they were donating blood—all these women were reclining back on these chairs. That was an interesting experience to look at all these women who had just been through what I had—all the various reactions. There was this woman on my left who was just sobbing and sobbing. I remember feeling like, I dealt with my emotions before and after the abortion, but on that day I felt like I just needed to be strong. I felt very exposed in that room, and felt uncomfortable that maybe I wasn't feeling guilty enough or emotional enough. I wish I could have talked to the women in the recovery area and all the people who worked there would just disappear. We were going through the same experience but we were totally isolated. They're giving you cookies and water and dealing with you on a physical level, but every woman in the room was going through an emotional experience, and none of us is going to turn to the person next to us and talk about it.

After the appointment my friends took me back to their place. It was a cozy apartment and we laid on the bed, watched cartoons, ate, and spent the whole afternoon hanging out. They were so gentle and just understood on a very basic level what they would feel like if they were in my shoes. I knew talking about it would be a long-term process, but on that day I just wanted to hang out on the bed and drink tea and talk girl talk.

There are certain arenas that are about women; I'm talking about experiences that are universal for women. I really felt that when I had my abortion, this was no-man's-land. This was woman's land. Even with a supportive partner, I feel overwhelmingly that it was the best decision I made to just stay with women that day. I think they understood in a way that no man could understand. I had made a deal with Hal that I would call him at a certain time. When that time came I felt really sad, I wasn't ready to deal. I was still in the process of taking care of myself and allowing myself to be taken care of.

My abortion is not at all something I take lightly. It wasn't "my right and I exercised it, damn it." It was really emotional, I definitely went through grieving. I remember when I found out I was pregnant and I put my hand on my belly and looking down and thinking, wow, it's a miracle to be a woman. But I also knew it was not a good time in my life to have a child—financially, emotionally, relationship-wise. I've read some women's perspectives who were very nonchalant about the whole experience. That blows my mind, because it just seems unreal that you could have the potential of giving life, and choose for very good reasons to not do that, but just walk away from that and feel completely nonchalant. That is not to say I'm wracked with guilt. I don't regret the decision. It's kind of like when you're in a really good relationship and it ends for good reasons. You're never going to regret having ended it but you're not going to regret having it in your life in the first place. It's like that—it's good, it's eye-opening, it teaches you things, and it's always with you.

Now that I'm older and at the age where I'm actually thinking about having a child, the thought that I had an abortion comes back to me sometimes and I wonder what happens if it comes time to have a child and I can't. That possibility plagues me. That's probably more paranoia than anything.

I never really felt the need to discuss it with my family, like when I got my period I never told anybody. I just looked up, grabbed a pad, slapped it on and said okay. Same with the abortion—I thought about it and made my decision and did it. At one time my mom and I were discussing abortion and she said, "But you wouldn't know about that," and she looked at me and I looked at her and she said, "Would you?" I said as a matter of fact I would. She said we could talk about it later. I don't know what she felt—maybe alienated because I never told her. My mom is pro-choice and everything, and we communicate really well, but we never brought it up again.

How to Find People to Support Your Decision

I didn't want to have a kid but I really was worried what everyone was going to think of me, my family and friends and the people I knew at church. I felt a lot of pressure. I was unhappy. My mother-in-law showed up on my front porch and started screaming at my husband to stop me from having an abortion. My best friend was with me. She just encouraged me to do what I wanted to do and be honest.

—SANDRA

No woman should have to deal alone with a problem as difficult as unwanted pregnancy, but it's hard to know sometimes whom to trust. We may long for unconditional support from our partner, our parents, our sisters and friends, but for many of us this just may not be available. We may worry, often realistically, that the people closest to us will be angry or judgmental if they find out that we were pregnant, or that they'll blab our secret to everyone in sight. Still worse, the people closest to us might want to pressure us to go one way or another with the pregnancy.

My boyfriend said it was my decision but . . . don't have the baby. He said, "If you're my friend, if you have feelings for me, you won't have this baby." I felt really sad and disappointed. I think he cared about me even though he didn't stay with me. We broke up soon after the abortion.

—INGRID

So although we don't want to be *too* trusting, we also don't want to be too paranoid, trying to deal with a tough situation without anyone's help. Unintended pregnancy can be emotionally painful enough, full of loneliness, grief, a sense of failed hopes, or a fear of losing control of our life. This kind of pain can change us in one of two ways: we can grow harder and more closed, or we can grow stronger and more loving. If we choose strength and love (and we do!) it's going to help to have a hand to guide us, a shoulder to cry on, and the warm heart of someone who loves us.

The ideal support person is someone who can take time to listen and be supportive of *all* options—who may suggest consequences of each option but not apply pressure to go one way or the other. The ideal support person will never tell our secret to people without our permission. So how do we predict who will give this kind of support? We can start by taking stock of how we think people close to us would react.

> *I had recently moved here and didn't have any friends. I didn't want to burden the father. We were close but in a casual relationship. We made love one time. I told him I was pregnant—I felt he had a right to know—but I said not to worry because I'd take care of everything. I drove myself to the clinic and drove home. It didn't seem odd to be so alone at the time, but it does now.*

—ELLIE

EXERCISE: HOW I THINK PEOPLE WOULD REACT

Think of all the people close to you—your boyfriend or husband, parents, friends, mothers of friends, family members, neighbors, teachers, people from your religious community, and coworkers. Write their names in one of the four columns that follow according to how you *think* they would react if you asked for their help at this time. (Don't include the names of young children or others who are not appropriate as support people for you.)

#1 People who I think would support me either way	#2 People who might support me either way	#3 People who would pressure me to continue the pregnancy	#4 People who would pressure me to have an abortion

Looking at Your List

Because we're trying to identify the best support people for you, the first people we will eliminate for now are those you put in columns three and four. These are the people who would probably pressure you one way or the other. You may not want to involve these people until you've made up your mind what you will do with your pregnancy, or you may not want to involve them at all.

Now let's look at the people in column one—those you think will support you no matter what you decide. Ask yourself this question: Will this person tell others about my situation, even if I ask them to keep it private?

If the answer is no and you trust this person (or these people) in column one with your secret, then you have just found yourself a support person.

If they are not trustworthy with your secret or if you have no one at all in column one, it's time to look at the people in column two. These are the people you might have to "feel out" a bit to see where they stand.

We had only been together about three months. We were very much in love and he was great through the whole process. He was very supportive and aware of hormonal changes that were going through me, and reminding me if I was crying that there were hormones zinging around. He and I did a lot of meditation together, trying to connect with the spirit of the child. We told it we really loved it, but soon we were going to ask it to leave.

—Lauren

Feeling Out a Person's Potential for Support

It might seem kind of sneaky (or stupid), but here are some scenarios to show you how you can feel out a person's opinions on abortion.

Scenario 1

Shiela: Guess what, Mom. This girl at school got kicked out of the house because her parents found out she had an abortion.

Mom: That's terrible. A girl that age getting pregnant!

(Uh-oh, could be trouble. Shiela's mom obviously disapproves of teen pregnancy.)

Shiela: I think it's terrible that they kicked her out. She was just trying to do the right thing. I mean, if she had a baby, how would she finish high school or get a job?

Mom: Well, it serves her right. If she's old enough to have sex then she's old enough to have a baby.

(Sure enough, this mother goes in column three—she'd probably pressure Shiela to continue her pregnancy. Unless Shiela decides that having

a baby is what she wants, she should probably not involve her mother right now.)

Scenario 2

LOIS: Oh, hi, Reverend Smith, I hope I'm not calling too late. But I just saw this thing on TV that said that members of our religion have the same abortion rate as everyone else!

SMITH: Well, I'm not surprised.

LOIS: So you think it's true? Doesn't the church say abortion is wrong?

SMITH: Yes, but that doesn't mean a lot of good people don't do things differently sometimes.

(A good sign . . .)

LOIS: Gee, that seems hypocritical.

SMITH: It may seem that way, but I try to have compassion for everyone's circumstances, not judgment. I think that's the most important job of the church.

(Good answer! This minister sounds like he can offer genuine support. Lois can put him in column one.)

All right, all right, you get the picture. . . .

PRACTICING HOW TO ASK FOR WHAT YOU NEED

Once you've picked who you'll tell, it helps to let them know clearly what you want from them at this time. The trouble is, the stress of an unintended pregnancy makes it tempting to fight and argue, to attack and accuse. This can make everything worse, put people on the defensive, and deepen our isolation and pain. The whole reason we're telling someone our secret is so that we have their companionship and love. If we ask for help in a loving and respectful way, we are more likely to get love, respect, and help in return.

How Not to Ask for Help	Effective Ways to Ask for Help
Making threats: "I'm going to tell you something, and if you tell anybody, so help me I'll kill you."	"There's something I want to talk to you about, but I need to know first that you're willing to keep this totally private."
Becoming invisible: "Nothing's wrong. Never mind."	"There's something I want to tell you, but I'm afraid you'll be angry. I'm hoping you can just be gentle for a minute so I can tell you what's going on."
Playing the loser: "I'm sorry. I hate to ask you this. I feel like such an idiot. You must be sick of me."	"You were so nice to me the last time I had a problem. Can I get your help with another one?"
Putting up a wall: "Shut up! Shut up! I don't give a damn what you want!"	"Right now I just need to think through my options. Can I just tell you what I'm thinking and have you listen?"
Avoiding responsibility: "Whatever. I don't care. It's up to you."	"Everyone is trying to tell me what to do. I was hoping you'd just listen and help me find my own answer."
Attacking: "Fine! We'll just kill it and pretend it never happened. Are you happy now?"	"I know you think I should have an abortion but could we just talk a little about what it would be like if we had this baby?"

My husband was not supportive. He wasn't very communicative. He seemed upset and I think he was resentful at me for having an abortion but he also didn't do anything to try to stop me. I think he also thought it was best.

—SANDRA

If You're Under Eighteen . . .

If you live in a state where teens who seek an abortion have to notify or get the consent of one or both parents (see "What Are the Laws in My State?" in Chapter Seven), you have a special reason to get the support of a parent now. Should you decide on an abortion, having a parent involved will make the process much simpler for you, at least legally.

Most teens do involve their parents in their decision process. Those who don't have many reasons, from concerns that they will be physically or emotionally abused by their parents to plain old fear of disappointing them.

If your fears are not of abuse or pressure but of anger and disappointment from your parents, think carefully whether these may be prices you can pay to have their support right now. You may find the experience brings you closer together.

If you do not want to involve your parents right now, it is a good idea to involve some other trusted adult. No matter what you decide to do about your pregnancy, there will be details, expenses, rides, and decisions necessary that can be made much easier with the help of a supportive adult.

I was so afraid I'd get kicked out of the house, I just didn't tell anyone. When the time came that I needed a ride to the clinic, I literally grabbed someone off the street.

—RITA

If You Fear Abuse

No one should risk abuse just because they are pregnant! You do not deserve to be hit, yelled at, or told you are a bad person no matter how you got pregnant and no matter what you decide to do. You are a good person and you deserve love and support. Love and support are the best medicine (the *only* medicine) when you are suffering from fear and indecision. If someone in your life has ever treated you abusively, it may be best not to tell them you are pregnant now.

Remember, all options—abortion, parenting, and adoption—are possible with or without the support or understanding of your parents, partner, or others. (In some states adoption requires the consent of the father, but if the father is abusive his right to stop the adoption can be denied.)

Counseling

Whether or not you find good support people in your life, counseling is a way to get professional help with your decision process. Most abortion providers have free or low-cost, short-term counseling available, or can tell you where to find it. When looking for pregnancy counseling, watch out for anti-abortion clinics that advertise free pregnancy counseling. These groups will pressure you not to have an abortion. For tips on recognizing and avoiding these groups, see "How to Avoid Fake Clinics" in Chapter Seven.

Privacy Counts!

Most women who consider having an abortion decide to keep their situations fairly private. In a more perfect world, we wouldn't have to fear so much gossip, judgment, and blame around our personal struggles, but this is often the case.

Of course, if you decide to continue your pregnancy your secret will eventually be impossible to keep. You can deal with this issue later (see Chapter Eight, "What to Do if You Want to Continue Your Pregnancy").

Privacy can also be a way to keep the decision process simpler. The more people who know about your pregnancy, the more you'll have to hear their opinions on what you should do. This can be confusing and the conflict can distract you from the very important decision you alone must ultimately make. Remember, your decision will affect you a hundred times more than it will affect them. So your opinion counts the most.

How Religious and Political Views of Abortion Affect You

What bothers me a lot is that a lot of people think if you're pro-choice it's nothing, and you just go have abortions and la-dee-da it doesn't mean anything to you. I honestly don't think that's women's experience.

—LISA

M ost of what we hear about abortion concerns the abortion "debate"—picketers, bombings, marches in Washington, bans on partial-birth procedures. These events get a lot of media attention but they don't have much to do with women's real abortion experiences. What is going on here? What is all the fuss about?

THE HISTORY OF ABORTION

Abortion has been with us at least as long as there has been recorded history. Women have always found the need for it and authorities have always had opinions about it, but it was usually accepted as a part of life.

Ancient Greek and Christian philosophers generally agreed that abortion was morally acceptable early in the pregnancy, before "quickening." Quickening was when they thought the fetus gained a soul, indicated by the woman's first sensations of fetal movement, which usually begin between the fourth and fifth months. The Catholic Church reversed its

65

position on abortion a number of times over the centuries, but in 1591 declared that abortion before quickening was only a venial sin and carried no penalties.

I don't believe women have to get pregnant. I think the power to conceive or not conceive is something we are meant to reclaim, but it's something we lost a long time ago. I don't think we're meant to be in this powerless position.

—LENA

For most of history, abortions, like most things related to pregnancy, were usually performed by women practitioners. Early methods for abortion included toxic douches, potions and suppositories, and the insertion of objects such as elm bark into the uterus.

In the United States, abortion was perfectly legal (and nothing women were ashamed of) before the mid-1800s. State laws at the time usually permitted abortion before quickening. After that, some laws prohibited certain methods of abortion, such as the use of dangerous poisons, because they endangered the life of the woman. But abortion tonics were advertised freely in magazines and newspapers as cures for "female trouble" and for late periods. Some researchers believe the abortion rate is about the same now as it has been for several hundred years (Luker, 1984).

In the 1850s, the newly established American Medical Association crusaded to outlaw abortion and to characterize women who ended their pregnancies as wicked and selfish. The doctors' motives were partly to protect women from the risks associated with any surgical procedure at the time. Making abortion a crime was also part of physicians' efforts to ruin the careers of female practitioners and midwives, however, so they could take over the practice of childbirth and women's reproductive health care services for themselves. As a result, abortion became illegal throughout the country except when a doctor decided it was appropriate—a judgment that varied from never to always, depending on the physician. About this time, the Pope also declared that abortion at any time during the pregnancy was a mortal sin (the serious kind). Abortion remained common and was simply performed illegally, though most people did not consider it a "real" crime.

By the 1950s, medicine had made leaps and bounds in the safety and effectiveness of surgical procedures, but abortion, hidden away in motel rooms, kitchens, and back alleys, remained a very dangerous procedure. Thousands of American women were hospitalized after illegal abortions; about a hundred died each year and many more were injured or made sterile. In addition, getting these illegal abortions forced women to travel long distances, pay huge amounts of money, and risk their personal safety in the hands of strangers.

With the landmark 1973 decision *Roe* v. *Wade,* the U.S. Supreme Court legalized abortion once again. Legalization rapidly increased the safety and technology of abortion, as doctors could finally publish and share developments in their techniques and providers could work in clean, well-equipped, licensed facilities.

Legalization also gave rise to today's anti-abortion movement, which has fought to ban and restrict abortion through many means. While most Americans today support a woman's right to have an abortion, many feel that some legal restrictions are necessary. Others feel that the government should never intrude upon a woman's right to decide for herself when and whether she will bear a child. These conflicts in our society have made abortion one of the most controversial issues of our time, and abortion providers have had to fight to keep abortion safe, legal, and accessible to all who need it.

> *It really is about power and powerlessness. The whole abortion debate is about pitting people against each other so they won't question who is really in power, which is men.*
>
> —LENA

THE POLITICS OF ABORTION

Most of what we hear about abortion concerns the battles waged between anti-abortion and pro-choice advocates on the sidewalks in front of clinics, in courtrooms, and on Capitol Hill. Although there are as many points of view as there are people, here is a basic rundown of the pro-choice and anti-abortion philosophies.

The Pro-Choice Point of View

The pro-choice movement believes that women must have access to safe, legal abortion. Because women's independence, health, and ability to earn a living are so closely tied to the timing of childbearing, pro-choice people believe it oppresses women to force them to bear children they do not want—and can be tragic for these children as well. Different pro-choice people have different ideas about when abortion is morally acceptable. Some believe it is the woman's choice under all circumstances, but most believe there are some moral limits that should be observed. Almost all pro-choice persons believe the more developed the fetus, the more serious the moral reason needed to justify abortion. Whether or not they believe the fetus is a "life," pro-choice people feel that, when forced to choose between consideration for the fetus and for the woman, the woman is more important. Some pro-choice people act on their beliefs by working in clinics that provide abortion, volunteering as clinic escorts, and working to change and protect laws to make abortion safer and more accessible.

The Anti-Abortion Point of View

The anti-abortion movement believes that abortion is murder and should never be performed (except, in some people's opinion, when it is necessary to save the woman's life or in cases of rape or incest). Many anti-abortion people think that easy availability of abortion encourages promiscuous sex and sex outside of marriage. They feel this undermines the sacredness of marriage and the family. Some anti-abortion people

In Good Conscience

hold similar views about birth control, feeling that God alone should decide when and whether a woman becomes pregnant. Some anti-abortion people act on their beliefs by offering support to women with unintended pregnancies. Others pray or picket outside clinics, or work politically to pass laws that restrict abortion access, such as informed consent or waiting period and parental consent or notification requirements described in Chapter Eight. Some anti-abortion people have gone so far as to block clinic entrances, vandalize and burn clinics, and commit other acts of violence, including murder.

A lot of picketers around here know me. We had to drive two hours away so I could get an abortion without them knowing about it. There was just one woman out there praying, and actually I was glad.

—ALLISON

Anti-Abortion Terrorism and Violence

Since the early 1980s, anti-abortion activity against abortion providers and clinics has increased. When anti-abortion people demonstrate peacefully outside clinics without directly interfering with the patient's ability to get in and out of the clinic, they are acting within their constitutional rights. However, individuals in the anti-abortion movement have committed acts of harassment and terrorism, including restraining people trying to enter the clinic, invading the clinic and locking everyone inside, destroying property at the clinic site, and, in hundreds of cases, bombing and burning clinics. Even worse, anti-abortion people have stalked clinic personnel and threatened their families. In 1993 and 1994, anti-abortion people in Canada and the United States, in four separate incidents, shot ten people who worked in abortion clinics. Five of the victims died. Law enforcement in various cities has not always been responsive to anti-abortion terrorism and violence, sometimes denying abortion providers the protection that would be offered to a hospital, home, or doctor's office in similar circumstances.

Under the Clinton administration, however, Congress has passed laws making stricter penalties against those who harass, terrorize, and commit violence against abortion providers and their clients. The FBI and Bureau of Alcohol, Tobacco and Firearms have increased their involvement, and clinics have increased their security.

It helped me to realize that God is life and God can't be killed.

—SANDRA

RELIGIOUS VIEWS OF ABORTION

You may be surprised to know that most religious groups actually support— or at least tolerate—a woman's right to choose abortion. Even in religions that are anti-abortion, there is often a wide gap between what religious leaders say and how members of the religion think and behave. For example, the Catholic Church has clearly declared abortion to be the worst kind of sin, yet one-third of all women who have abortions are Catholic. They have an abortion rate 29 percent higher than other Christian women, and they support women's right to choose abortion at the same rate as other Americans. Women who describe themselves as born-again or evangelical Christians account for almost one in five U.S. abortions. In short, people in all religions have abortions, and most religious Americans are pro-choice.

I grew up in a fundamentalist Christian family. We believed that abortion was killing someone, and since I was a good person, I never thought I would be in that situation. But there was just no way I could have a baby at that time. I was sure the hand of God was going to come down and take my soul.

—*Sarah*

Among religious communities with official pro-choice positions are nearly all Protestant denominations, including the American Baptist

Church, the United Church of Christ, the Episcopal Church, the Presbyterian Church, the United Methodists, and the Unitarian Universalists. The United Synagogue of Conservative Judaism and the Union of American Hebrew Congregations are also pro-choice.

In making their statements, most of these groups acknowledge diversity of opinion among their members, and many express mixed feelings about supporting choice. For example, the American Baptist Church writes: "As American Baptists we oppose abortion as a means of avoiding responsibility for conception [and] as a primary means of birth control, without regard for the far reaching consequences of the act. We denounce irresponsible sexual behavior and acts of sexual violence that contribute to the large number of abortions each year. We grieve with all who struggle with the difficult circumstances that lead them to consider abortion. Recognizing that each person is ultimately responsible to God, we encourage women and men in these circumstances to seek spiritual counsel as they prayerfully and conscientiously consider their decision" (General Board, 1988).

My mother made me stand up in front of the whole church and confess to everyone that I had an abortion. Here's my mother saying if I didn't repent I was going to go to Hell and I figured I was going to Hell anyway. That's where I stopped believing in God.

—RITA

Others, such as the American Jewish Committee, emphasize the immorality of government involvement: "While Jewish tradition on this issue is complex, it allows for various options depending on individual cases and circumstances. The obvious lack of religious and civic consensus on this subject only underscores the importance of government not imposing one particular view of abortion on those of diverse religious and ethnic backgrounds. Such a position is consistent with not only Jewish tradition but also pro-family values and the rights and dignity of women" (Religious Coalition for Reproductive Choice, 1996).

Who Is Pro-Choice?

The following religious organizations have formally made statements supporting the right and recognizing the necessity to choose abortion.

- American Baptist Churches
- American Ethical Union
- American Friends Service Committee
- American Humanist Association
- American Jewish Committee
- Jewish Women International (formerly B'nai Brith Women)
- Central Conference of American Rabbis
- Christian Church (Disciples of Christ)
- Council of Jewish Federations
- Episcopal Church
- Episcopal Women's Caucus
- Federation of Reconstructionist Congregations and Havurot
- Lutheran Women's Caucus
- Moravian Church in America, Northern Province
- NA'AMAT USA
- National Council of Jewish Women
- Women of Reform Judaism
- North American Federation of Temple Youth
- Presbyterian Church (United States)
- Reorganized Church of Jesus Christ of Latter Day Saints
- Union of American Hebrew Congregations
- Unitarian Universalist Association
- United Church of Christ
- United Methodist Church

- United Synagogue for Conservative Judaism
- Women's American ORT
- Women's League for Conservative Judaism
- Young Women's Christian Association of the United States

If you don't see your religious group represented here, don't assume they are against abortion. For information about the positions of groups listed above, or to find out about other religious groups' positions on abortion, contact the Religious Coalition for Reproductive Choice at (202) 628-7700. Or call your local church, synagogue, temple, or mosque.

How to Make the Right Decision: Write-In Section on Your Life, Feelings, and Spiritual Beliefs

At this point you may feel definite about what you'll do about your pregnancy. For many women, however, there is some ambivalence—a feeling of being torn or not quite right with any decision. This chapter is a place for you to reflect and write about your own feelings and your own conscience. It is not intended to change your mind, but you may want to be open to that possibility while you write in this book. The best imaginable outcome for you is that you feel clear about your decision now and in the future. My wish for you—and that of everyone who faces this important choice—is that you will always look back on this decision and feel that you did the best thing for you.

If working through the emotional and spiritual aspects of your decision is something you feel would be helpful, try to set aside quiet time to reflect and write about the following questions. You may want to spend some time alone, take a long walk, pray, or meditate—whatever helps you think more clearly in times of confusion.

Feel free to use extra paper when you need to, but don't feel like you have to write a book. Short answers that fit in the spaces provided will help you get more perspective than you might think. If the questions seem stupid or irrelevant, you don't have to answer them. But sometimes a dumb question will bring up an answer that changes your insight. You may also want to share your written thoughts with a support person, counselor, or your partner.

To remind you that you are not alone, workbook sections say "we" and "us" in describing the decision process. The information and questions in these sections are based on the experience of hundreds of women who faced the abortion decision, including those interviewed for this book.

LEARNING YOU ARE PREGNANT

For many of us, finding out we were pregnant was a horrible discovery. We may have suspected a pregnancy even before our period was late—because we had unprotected sex, because we started feeling the early symptoms of pregnancy, or because we intuitively "knew." A few of us were happy about the pregnancy, but later, for health reasons, a change in our relationship with the male partner, or some other reason, we realized carrying the pregnancy to term might not be best.

Some of us used home pregnancy tests, others went to a clinic or a doctor's office, waiting on pins and needles to learn the results of the test. We thought back anxiously to remember the day when conception must have occurred. Whether we felt happy, fearful, or a mixture of feelings, this was often the beginning of a stressful time.

- What made you suspect you were pregnant?

  _____

- How did you learn that you were definitely pregnant?

  _____

- How did you feel when you found out?

  _____

  _____

  _____

• How did this pregnancy occur?

_____

_____

_____

SOURCES OF SUPPORT

Unintended pregnancy is something few of us could bear alone, and often we carefully chose the people in our lives with whom we would share the truth. Sometimes these people were supportive, others turned out to be critical and judgmental, even threatening. Some of us were afraid to tell the people closest to us for fear they would be disappointed or reject us. Still, it was important that we told *someone* who could support us no matter what we decided.

• List the people in your life who know that you are pregnant, and rate on a scale of one to ten the level of support they are giving you.

_____

_____

_____

• What kinds of feelings have they expressed about the fact that you're pregnant?

_____

_____

_____

• List the people in your life whom you feel you cannot tell, and why.

_____

_____

_____

• Who in your life has experienced abortion before?

_____

_____

_____

• How did they describe the experience?

_____

_____

_____

• Who in your life can give you unconditional support, no matter what you decide?

_____

_____

_____

- What steps can you take to get support from those people?

_____

_____

_____

- What are your options for professional counseling? Would counseling be helpful to you now?

_____

_____

_____

PHYSICAL HEALTH

Pregnancy was a physically uncomfortable time for many of us. We may have felt exhausted and fat, emotional and nauseated. Some of us craved huge meals and others wanted to throw up even thinking of food. Worst of all, we felt extreme stress every day because we were pregnant when we didn't want to be. This stress can make things even worse, causing us to lose sleep, become depressed or "hyper," eat badly and even get into—or increase—addictive behavior. We found that it helped to focus our attention on taking care of our bodies.

- In what ways are you taking care of yourself right now (sleep, food, exercise, recreation, spiritual life)?

_____

_____

_____

• In what ways could you improve the way you take care of yourself?

_____

_____

_____

• What symptoms of pregnancy are bothering you today?

_____

_____

_____

• Are you able to avoid using drugs, tobacco, and alcohol right now? If not, why not?

_____

_____

_____

• What are some things you can do to nurture your body, mind, and spirit at this time?

_____

_____

_____

FEELINGS ABOUT PREGNANCY

It is common to feel a mixture of feelings about pregnancy—excitement, happiness to know we are fertile, love for the potential child, hope about our relationship with our male partner—but negative feelings like fear and anger are often there too. Sometimes we couldn't face it all at once and we wanted to blank it out or pretend it wasn't happening. When we don't face our real problems, it's called denial. Denial is dangerous during an unintended pregnancy. Unless we faced our dilemma head-on, we couldn't make a conscious decision about what is best for us.

- Are you tempted to go into denial about the decision you face? How can you avoid denial?

_____

_____

_____

- Do you have negative feelings about this pregnancy? What are they?

_____

_____

_____

- Do you have positive feelings about this pregnancy? What are they?

_____

_____

_____

- If you continued this pregnancy, how do you imagine you'd feel about it at six months? Nine months?

  _____

  _____

  _____

- How do you imagine you would feel if the pregnancy were interrupted by abortion?

  _____

  _____

  _____

- List all the ways you have successfully prevented pregnancy in the past.

  _____

  _____

  _____

FEELINGS ABOUT CHILDREN

For many of us, an unintended pregnancy—even if we planned to end it with abortion—brought up thoughts of children. Whether we already had children or we hoped to have a child sometime in the future, we needed to think through what it would mean if we were to raise a brand-new baby now.

- Do you wish to have a child at some time in the future? What would you like your life to be like when you raise that child?

  _____

  _____

  _____

- How well does your current situation match the situation you'd like to have for yourself and your child?

  _____

  _____

  _____

- Do you have fears about your future ability to have children? Why?

  _____

  _____

  _____

- If you already have children, how would a new baby affect them?

  _____

  _____

  _____

- Could you continue your current work or school commitments during a pregnancy? After a child was born?

_____

_____

_____

- Do you feel secure that this is a healthy pregnancy? Why or why not?

_____

_____

_____

FEELINGS ABOUT ABORTION

Most of us grew up hearing hot debates about abortion in the media, and may have had parents and other influential people in our lives who had strong opinions on whether abortion was right or wrong. When we considered abortion for ourselves, we needed to sort out our own feelings, separate from others' opinions. Some of us were against abortion until we found out we were pregnant. Others of us who were solidly pro-choice thought that abortion might not be the best choice for ourselves personally. Some had had an abortion in the past, and though we promised ourselves we would never let it happen again, we felt abortion was again the best choice. Whatever we decided, our decision affected us more than anyone else, so the decision had to be our own.

- How did you feel about abortion before you got pregnant?

_____

_____

_____

- If you have had an abortion before, how did you feel about it at that time?

  _____

  _____

  _____

- What are your parents' attitudes about abortion?

  _____

  _____

  _____

- Is it important to you to share your parents' attitudes?

  _____

  _____

  _____

- Did you and your partner discuss how you each felt about abortion before you were pregnant?

  _____

  _____

  _____

• Have your feelings changed now? Have his?

_____

_____

_____

FEELINGS ABOUT ADOPTION

Adoption today can be a lot easier for everyone involved than it was in the past, but many women consider it the most difficult choice. Only about 3 percent of unintended pregnancies result in adoption, mostly because it takes a great deal of commitment to carry a pregnancy to term and then place the baby with another family. Still, most women who opt for adoption feel good about their decision, and many have contact with the child and his or her adoptive family.

• How did you feel about adoption before you were pregnant? Is it something you would consider now?

_____

_____

_____

• Do you know people who placed children for adoption? Who adopted children? Who are adopted? How do they feel about this?

_____

_____

_____

- If adoption were your choice, would you prefer an open adoption, where the biological mother has contact with the child and the adoptive family, or a closed adoption, where the biological mother remains anonymous and has no contact?

  _____

  _____

  _____

- Does the possibility of receiving money for pregnancy expenses make adoption a better alternative than it would be otherwise?

  _____

  _____

  _____

- Could you continue your current work or school commitments during a pregnancy and until an adoption took place?

  _____

  _____

  _____

- What kind of adoptive parents would you want for the child?

  _____

  _____

  _____

LIFE GOALS

One of the most common reasons that women choose abortion is because the potential child would seriously affect their goals in life. Those of us who are in high school or college know that parenthood would probably require postponing our education for several years. Women who work outside the home worry about how they would afford child care or whether they'd be able to keep their jobs at all. Still other women worry that it will be harder to find a life partner as a single mother.

The fact is that some of us in the most difficult circumstances have successfully raised children, completed our education, held good jobs, and succeeded both as single moms and as married moms. Although these successes are possible, it is more often true that mothers—especially low-income and single mothers—must sacrifice some education, work, and personal goals in order to raise a child.

An unintended pregnancy can be very stressful, and under so much pressure it was sometimes hard to think realistically about how a child would really have an impact on our lives. Thinking realistically is very, very important now. Caring for a baby or a young child is a full-time job, and unless we had commitments from our partner or family members to give us lots of help with finances and child care, many of us faced the fact that we might be caring for the child by ourselves.

• What are your most important goals right now?

_____

_____

_____

- Realistically, how would having a baby affect these goals?

  _____

  _____

  _____

- How would you financially handle it if you were to have this baby and raise it?

  _____

  _____

- Do you have a partner who will share the responsibility?

  _____

  _____

  _____

- Do you feel secure that he will fulfill that responsibility? Why or why not?

  _____

  _____

  _____

FEELINGS ABOUT THE MAN INVOLVED

An unintended pregnancy can bring up very strong feelings about our male partner, and many of us were forced to explore difficult questions about our relationship, our hopes and dreams for it, and the reality of what we could really expect. Some of us receive strong and unconditional support from these men, but others get no support at all. Some of us choose not to tell the man that we are pregnant, which is also our right.

Many of us felt that our decision depended upon how the man reacted to the pregnancy, and whether he would promise to be there for us and help us raise the potential child. For this reason, it was critical to think realistically about the relationship. Because no relationship is guaranteed, we also had to think through how we would live if we were raising a child and the relationship ended.

In some cases, we disagreed with our partner about whether or not to end the pregnancy. Sometimes this was painful for us and harmful to our relationships. We wanted to consider the man's feelings in our decisions, but we knew that whatever we chose it would affect us more than it would him. Ultimately, we had to make the decision that was best for us.

- How do you feel about the man who shares responsibility for this pregnancy?

  _____

  _____

  _____

- Would you like him to be in your life a year from now?

  _____

- If you are not married, is marriage a possibility?

  _____

- How would you like the relationship to be?

  _____

  _____

  _____

- List the negative aspects of your relationship with the man.

  _____

  _____

  _____

- List the positive aspects of your relationship with the man.

  _____

  _____

  _____

- How do you feel your relationship with your partner would be affected by the birth of a baby?

  _____

  _____

  _____

- How do you feel the relationship would be affected by an abortion?

  _____

  _____

  _____

- Will your partner support you no matter what you decide?

  _____

- Does he plan to remain as your partner no matter what you decide?

  _____

- What could he do now to support you?

  _____

  _____

  _____

FEELINGS ABOUT SEX

It is fairly common for us to have confusion or mixed feelings about sex. We live in a culture that has no clear definition of healthy sexuality, a fact that strongly affects women, and young women in particular. Many of us grew up with mixed messages that gave us the feeling that if we weren't having sex we were somehow losers. Yet if we were having sex, some people considered us bad or "slutty." This confusion was a factor that led many of us to have unprotected sex. Many of us thought that using birth control made us look like we were "expecting" sex.

Unhappy feelings about sex can cause serious problems in all areas of our lives, and sometimes can lead us to become pregnant when we don't want to be. Still, the pregnancy can be an opportunity to look at how confusion about sex has harmed us, to heal those wounds, and to treat our own sexuality with new care and respect.

- What are your feelings about your sexual relationship?

  _____

  _____

  _____

- Are there any aspects of your sex life that cause you negative feelings?

  _____

  _____

  _____

- What in your sex life causes positive feelings?

  _____

  _____

  _____

- Are there any ways that bad feelings like guilt, shame, fear, or anger might be influencing your thinking right now?

  _____

  _____

  _____

- What experiences of sex led to any negative feelings you may have?

  _____

  _____

  _____

- Is sexual abuse a part of your past? If so, is this affecting you now?

  _____

  _____

  _____

- At the time you became pregnant, was sex a healthy thing for you?

  _____

  _____

  _____

- Are there aspects of your sex life you'd like to change?

  _____

  _____

  _____

- What is your ideal sexual relationship?

  _____

  _____

  _____

- Are there ways you can begin to heal sexual hurts from the past?

_____

_____

_____

RELIGIOUS BELIEFS

If we were religious (or if we were raised in a religious family) many of us contemplated our unplanned pregnancy in terms of our religious traditions and beliefs. Most religions in the United States acknowledge that abortion is sometimes the morally right decision for a woman (see the final section of Chapter Five for a list of religions that support abortion). Those of us who had support from our religious group, no matter what we decided to choose, found it a great comfort.

Others of us practiced one of the religions that condemn abortion. Because these religions tend also to condemn sex outside of marriage and even birth control, many of us facing an unintended pregnancy already felt conflicted about how closely we would stick to our religious traditions. It helped to know that abortion is common among women of all religions, regardless of what their church teaches. Ultimately, those of us who were religious had to weigh the importance of our religious teachings with what felt right in our hearts.

- If you were raised within a certain religion, what are its teachings about abortion?

_____

_____

_____

- How do you feel about most of the teachings of your religion?

  _____

  _____

  _____

- If you had an abortion, do you feel you could continue to participate in your religion as you wish?

  _____

- Would you have to hide the fact that you had an abortion? Why?

  _____

  _____

  _____

- If you had a baby now, do you feel you could continue to participate in your religion as you wish?

  _____

- Is there a person within your religion whom you could confide in and find unconditional support?

  _____

SPIRITUAL BELIEFS

Whether or not we took part in a religion, almost all of us had some kind of strong and personal sense of spirituality. Whether we conceived of it as God, the earth, the greater good, an inner knowing, the magic of life itself, or some other form of Higher Power, many of us had strong spiritual beliefs in something greater than our day-to-day selves that guided us in our decisions in life.

- Do you believe you are guided by a Higher Power, such as God, Goddess, the universe, nature, your higher self, or the collective conscience?

  _____

- What is your relationship to that Higher Power?

  _____

  _____

  _____

- How do you imagine your Higher Power sees your pregnancy?

  _____

  _____

  _____

- Trust for a moment that you have a loving Higher Power who always wants what is best for you. In what ways do you "hear" your Higher Power's wishes for you?

  _____

  _____

  _____

- Do you have a sense of connection now to your Higher Power?

  _____

- In what ways do you find connection?

  _____

  _____

  _____

Suggested Spiritual Exercises

1. Keep a journal of your experiences every day, noting both the positive and negative feelings you experience, thoughts about your decision or dreams.

2. Take meditation walks—time alone to think, breathe, and relax.

3. If more connection with your Higher Power is what you seek, write a prayer as often as you need to, asking for guidance as you make this decision.

4. Calm your mind with meditation. Sit quietly for ten minutes, silently focusing on a word that is positive for you, such as "peace," "good," "Jesus," or just a sound that helps soothe your mind.

5. Make a "God Box," a place to put pieces of paper where you have written things that you are asking your Higher Power to take care of for you.

6. Write a letter to your Higher Power explaining your situation and asking for guidance. Turn the piece of paper over, empty your mind, and write a letter back from your Higher Power.

7. Make a forgiveness list. Write, "I forgive (name)" for everyone you are ready to forgive, beginning with yourself.

SORTING OUT YOUR FEELINGS

The table that follows provides a place to write down your positive and negative feelings about various aspects of this pregnancy. For example, next to "People supporting you" one might write "relieved that Mom knows" under Good Feelings and "Afraid boyfriend will insist on abortion" under bad feelings. Feel free to add your own issues at the bottom of the left-hand column. When you're done, review these lists; look for patterns in each column.

Sorting Out Your Feelings.

	Good Feelings	Bad Feelings
Learning you are pregnant		
People supporting you		
Physical health		
Feelings about children		
Feelings about abortion		
Feelings about adoption		
Feelings about the man involved		
Feelings about sex		
Other feelings		

What to Do if Abortion
Is Your Choice

*I was brought up by a single mother, African-American, in the '50s
and '60s in a working-class town. I have a different way of looking at
life. I was brought up to have a sense of responsibility. I saw my
mother make a lot of sacrifices, and I'm not a martyr like that. She's
always manipulating us with this "I sacrificed for my children," and
I am not going to do that.*

—NAOMI

If you're pretty sure you want to end your pregnancy, you'll need to plan
how you will pay for the procedure and you'll need to make an appointment with an abortion provider.

PAYING FOR THE ABORTION

There are several possibilities.

Paying Cash

If your abortion is not covered by insurance, a first-trimester procedure will cost between $300 and $350 at a clinic. Hospitals and private
doctors sometimes charge more. The cost rises as the pregnancy continues, with second-trimester abortions costing as much as $2,500 and more.
The best thing you can do to keep the cost low is to schedule your abortion early in the pregnancy.

Abortion Providers

An abortion provider is a place or person who performs abortions. Sometimes it is a hospital, sometimes it is a private doctor's office, sometimes it is a clinic with lots of other services, and sometimes it is a clinic that only provides abortions.

Pro-Choice Providers

Some hospitals, doctors, and clinics do not provide abortion, but they will help you connect with a provider that does. If you don't live near an abortion provider, you can still get some services from a pro-choice provider, including pregnancy testing and counseling.

Private Insurance

The good news is, most private insurance covers abortion services. The bad news is, they are not always good at protecting your privacy from parents, spouses, or other family members on your insurance policy. If you know workers on staff at the facility where you will receive the abortion, keep in mind that they usually have access to service records as well. If authorization or confidentiality issues present a problem for you, you may wish to consider paying cash for your abortion.

The second possible problem with insurance is that you may face long delays in getting an abortion scheduled and authorized. For these reasons, a good first step if you have private insurance is to call your regular doctor (or the insurance company) and ask how they handle the abortion process. You don't have to give your name. Using insurance can save you a lot of money, but it can cause a lot of headache. You always have the option of going outside your insurance and paying cash.

Medicaid

Medicaid is federal health insurance for low-income people, including some teenagers who don't have private insurance. In California this insurance is called MediCal. As with all Medicaid funding, you must prove you are eligible, and to do this you have to talk to an eligibility worker.

Fifteen states use Medicaid funding for abortion no matter what your reasons for choosing abortion. These states are Alaska, California, Connecticut, Hawaii, Idaho, Illinois, Massachusetts, Minnesota, Montana, New Jersey, New York, Oregon, Vermont, Washington, and West Virginia. If you can prove with identification that you live in one of these states, talk to a Medicaid eligibility worker right away. Medicaid is confidential and can usually authorize you within a week.

Things to Bring When You Apply for Medicaid

When you meet with a Medicaid eligibility worker, you will need to bring the following.

1. Photo identification
2. Social security card or number
3. Proof of income including stubs from checks you've received from employment or public assistance
4. A pregnancy verification form, available from doctors and clinics where pregnancy tests are performed. You will have to have a pregnancy test at the clinic or doctor's office to receive this form. Family planning clinics such as Planned Parenthood offer this test free or at low cost. Call in advance to find out the cost.

All states NOT among the fifteen just listed DO NOT use Medicaid to pay for abortion, except when the pregnancy could endanger the woman's life or (usually) in cases of rape or incest. These laws can change quickly. For current information on your state, call your local abortion provider.

If You Are Uninsured and Have No Money . . .

In states where Medicaid covers abortion, you may be eligible for emergency Medicaid coverage. This coverage will pay for your abortion but will be stopped afterward.

If Medicaid coverage is not available to you, you will have to scrape the cash together somehow. Some women are eligible for grants, discounts, and payment plans through local clinics or from private funders. For information about this funding, call your provider or call the National Abortion Federation at 1-800-772-9100.

No matter what, you should never continue a pregnancy simply because you don't have cash for an abortion. Keep calling. Keep trying. Ask friends for help. Remember, childbirth is going to cost you a lot more in the long run than an abortion will cost you today.

> *The nurse midwife who gave me my test results said I should think carefully about my decision, and I remember riding my bike home from there and crying profusely because I knew what I was going to do.*
>
> —INGRID

MAKE AN APPOINTMENT

The next thing you should do is call an abortion provider and make an appointment. If possible, get an appointment within the first twelve weeks of pregnancy, when risks and costs are low. Remember, you can always postpone or cancel your appointment if you're not ready. But it can take a long time to get an appointment—and there can be a lot of hassles you'll have to go through first—so start the process early.

How to Find a Provider

When looking for abortion providers, there are three simple steps you can take.

1. **Look in the yellow pages under "Abortion."** (Watch out for fake clinics, usually listed under the heading "Abortion Alternatives.")

2. **If you don't see any listings for abortion,** or even if you do but you want to make sure they're good providers, call the National Abortion Federation hotline at 1-800-772-9100. This hotline is staffed by people who can help you with all aspects of abortion—when you're looking for a provider, when you need information, or when you just need to talk. The line is open from 9:30 A.M. to 5:30 P.M. Eastern Time (that's 6:30 A.M. to 2:30 P.M. on the West Coast and somewhere in between in the middle states).

3. **To get hooked up directly to a clinic,** call Planned Parenthood at 1-800-230-PLAN. This number will connect you with the nearest Planned Parenthood clinic. Though not all clinics provide abortion, they can give you all the information and referrals you need. Most clinics are only open weekdays between about 9:00 in the morning and 5:00 at night, though some have later and weekend hours.

I had two abortions with my ex-husband. He was a very abusive man and I didn't want to bring any more children into his life.

—RITA

How to Avoid Fake Clinics

Although some area Yellow Pages have cracked down on the practice, a number of anti-abortion organizations use advertising designed to trick you into calling them for abortion services. Once they get you in the door, they will try to pressure you to have a baby. They will give you lectures, show you films of aborted fetuses and stillborn babies, and even lie to you just to stop you from having an abortion. Of course, they won't help you find an abortion provider (see "Crisis Pregnancy Centers" in Chapter Eight).

Not all anti-abortion facilities are dishonest. Some will tell you up front that they are against abortion and wish to support you in carrying the pregnancy to term. But unless you *want* this type of service, it is best to use facilities that will support you whatever you decide. Remember that abortion providers are pro-choice—they are there to help you choose the option that is best for you, whether it's abortion, adoption, or raising the baby yourself.

> *Part of me really wanted those kids. I still think of how old they would be. I almost certainly won't have kids now, though now I could raise a child properly. I wish there was some way I could have taken those three pregnancies and put them on hold.*

> —LISA

Avoiding Anti-Abortion Groups

If you wish to avoid anti-abortion organizations, watch for these signs in the Yellow Pages or other advertising.

- No clear statement that abortion is provided
- Vague statements such as "Pregnant? We Can Help" or "Let's Talk About Your Options" or "Is Abortion What You Really Want?"
- A facility name that includes "Crisis Pregnancy" in its name
- Any facility listed under the heading "Abortion Alternatives," a heading created by the Yellow Pages people to separate fake abortion providers from real ones

When you call organizations, use the following strategies.

- Ask the receptionist directly if they provide abortion or if they can refer you to a place that does. If she does not say yes in a direct way, hang up and check the clinic's legitimacy with the National Abortion Federation.
- Watch out if the receptionist starts to ask you a lot of personal questions that don't have to do with abortion or early pregnancy, or if they refer to your pregnancy as a "baby."

- If the receptionist won't answer your questions about the clinic's abortion services over the phone and insists you need to come in and talk, hang up and call the National Abortion Federation.

The main factor was that I couldn't take care of a child and the father couldn't take care of the child without it destroying both of our lives.

—ELLIE

Choosing a Provider: Things to Ask

If you have more than one abortion provider to choose from, here are questions to ask to get the basic information you need and to see which one is best for you.

- Do you perform abortions?
- What days are abortion services available?
- How soon do you have openings?
- Are there restrictive laws I'll have to deal with, and can you help me with the process? (See "Laws Restricting Abortion" and "What Are the Laws in My State," both later in this chapter.)
- What is the cost of an abortion at my stage of pregnancy?
- What payment methods are available?
- When does the cost go up?
- Do you help with eligibility, funding, and insurance paperwork?
- What kinds of anesthesia are available?
- Are there any extra charges for tests or drugs?
- Are partners or friends allowed in the room?
- Are children allowed to come to the clinic?
- Is help with child care or transportation available?
- Can I expect picketers to be outside? How should I deal with them?

- Can you meet special needs, such as a language interpreter or disability access?
- Is birth control available after the procedure? Which methods?

I got pregnant the first week I was married and I was going to have the baby and I told everybody about it in my family and in church. And then I realized I just didn't get along with this person I married, and I already had a son and I could see I was going to be on my own again.

—SANDRA

THE DAY OF YOUR ABORTION

Once you make an appointment, your provider will give you detailed instructions on how to prepare for your abortion visit and what to expect. If you are having a second-trimester abortion, or if you live in a state with informed consent or waiting period laws (see "Laws Restricting Abortion" later in this chapter), you will probably have to visit the clinic before the day of your abortion as well. But the following are some general tips for the day of the procedure.

- Wear loose, comfortable clothing.
- Have something to eat before you come, as you will be at the clinic for several hours.
- Do not bring children.
- Tell your doctor in advance of any regular medication you take.
- Do not use any other drugs, including alcohol, as you may not be legally allowed to give your consent to the procedure if you are intoxicated.
- Bring a support person if you can, at least to drive you home. If you are given any narcotic pain medication, you will have to have someone else drive you home.

- Be prepared to take the remainder of the day off, though if you must, you can return to work.

PICKETERS

With stronger laws now in force against people who threaten and assault abortion providers, picketing is more popular than ever. When you make an appointment, your abortion provider will tell you whether you can expect picketers and the best ways to deal with them at that site. But here are some rules of thumb.

Picketers can scream, yell, show you ugly pictures, and make you very uncomfortable, but by law they can't actually touch you. The law does allow picketers to be on most sidewalks, but more and more clinics now have their entrances in the backs of buildings and in their parking lots, away from sidewalks. These entrances create a zone of private property where you can park but picketers must stay away.

Picketers have different motives. Some are simply outside clinics to pray. Others hold signs to raise awareness of their concerns about abortion. Many will shout at women entering clinics—some begging women not to have an abortion, some asking them to come over and talk, a few offering support for alternatives to abortion. But there are usually one or more troublemakers who delight in humiliating women and making a big, embarrassing scene. By all means, if you feel bad about your decision and these anti-abortion messages are something you want to hear, it's okay to talk to the picketers. Keep in mind, though, that their goal is to stop you from having an abortion, so if you talk to them and then go ahead with your appointment, they may increase their shouting, begging, and humiliating behavior.

If you do not feel that you will benefit from talking with the picketers, *ignore them*. Don't get into a conversation with them, even to yell back at them. It's not as though they haven't heard all your arguments before. They want you to argue with them because it helps them get *your* attention.

No matter what, *do not touch picketers.* If you touch them they can have you arrested. If you get arrested, they have successfully stopped you from having an abortion.

If you feel upset by what you heard or saw outside, tell the receptionist inside and she will make sure counseling is available to you.

> *What I was afraid of was poverty. I was afraid I'd have to go on aid to have kids.*
>
> —LISA

LAWS RESTRICTING ABORTION

Increasingly, states are adopting laws that restrict access to abortion. Parental involvement, waiting period, and informed consent laws tend to make it difficult for you to get an abortion. That's exactly what they are designed to do. When you make an appointment, your provider will tell you which laws are in place in your state and they will help you comply with those laws.

Parental Consent and Notification

More than half the states enforce parental involvement laws that require women under the age of eighteen who seek an abortion to get the consent of—or prove that they notified—one or both parents. (Ask your provider or check "What Are the Laws in My State?" to see which laws, if any, your state enforces.) Depending on the state, these laws can be quite complicated. Sometimes your parents have to come into the clinic, sometimes you just need to bring in notarized paperwork. Sometimes one parent is enough, sometimes they want two, even when one of your parents is who-knows-where. Sometimes any adult can sign for you, and sometimes doctors will waive the requirement altogether. Your provider can work with you to help you meet the requirements in your state.

Most teens involve their parents in their abortion decision without such laws. Teens who don't involve them say they don't want to hurt their parents, and others mention problems at home, including physical and sexual abuse, as reasons why parental involvement is impossible. All states with these restrictions must provide a judicial bypass—a way for a teen who can't or won't involve her parents to get a court order saying she can have an abortion.

In a judicial bypass, a teenager meets with a judge who talks with her and determines whether she is mature enough to make the abortion decision on her own and whether the abortion is in her best interests. The teenager usually has a court-appointed lawyer or advocate, and often works with a social worker as well. The whole process can take a week, but does not cost anything for the teen. The judge is in a position where he or she must determine that either the girl is mature enough and may go ahead with her plan, or that she is not mature enough and must therefore involve her parents (who may then force her to become a parent). No matter how they feel about abortion, almost all judges avoid this problem and approve all requests for abortion. Even if they don't, you can almost always win on appeal. Some judges, however, are against abortion and use this opportunity to embarrass the teenager and put her down.

If you are a teenager in a parental involvement state, it is recommended that you skip this crazy courtroom thing and involve your parents if you possibly can. Having adults involved can take a lot of the stress out of abortion—including how you'll get there, how you'll pay for it, and how you'll hide it from everyone. If you feel you just can't involve them, follow your instincts. Your provider will help you initiate the judicial bypass process by connecting you with a pro-choice attorney or teen advocate. Either the provider, the attorney, or the advocate will help you do the following.

- File the paperwork
- Plan what to say and what to wear
- Keep the process confidential
- Cope with the stress of the courts

Informed Consent and Waiting Period Requirements

To date, thirty states have adopted informed consent and waiting period requirements for women of any age who want an abortion. These laws require a woman to hear state-scripted warnings and lectures designed to make her decide against abortion. These lectures (sometimes recordings or videos) explain that parenting and adoption are also options, and often describe government programs available to pregnant and parenting women. Some states also require that women be offered anti-abortion brochures and pictures or videos on fetal development. All of this information is available from providers anyway, who must give complete information about the risks and benefits of all medical procedures, with or without these special laws.

Most informed consent laws go hand in hand with waiting period requirements, where women have to wait twenty-four hours or more after hearing the lecture before actually getting the abortion. This can be a big pain for everyone concerned, but it can be a serious problem for women who have to take time off work, travel long distances, or get child care for their visits to the clinic. Your provider can advise you on the best way to comply with these laws.

I Don't Understand These Laws!

For more detailed information on laws that restrict abortion and how to comply with them, contact the following:

- Your abortion provider
- Planned Parenthood at 1-800-230-PLAN (or at http://www.planned-parenthood.org)
- The National Abortion Federation at 1-800-772-9100 (or at http://www.prochoice.org/naf)

Another great resource on restrictive laws and other abortion-related information is *The Abortion Resource Handbook* (Kaufman, 1997), available in bookstores.

State	Informed Consent/ Waiting Period	Parental Consent/ Notification	Medicaid Coverage
Alabama	No	One-parent consent/judicial bypass	Life endangerment only
Alaska	No	Not enforced	Yes
Arizona	No	Not enforced	Life endangerment, rape, and incest only
Arkansas	No	Two-parent notification with 48-hour waiting period or judicial bypass	Life endangerment, rape, and incest only
California	No	Not enforced	Yes
Colorado	No	Not enforced	Life endangerment, rape, and incest only
Connecticut	No	Counseling on options and possibility of parental involvement required for minors under 16	Yes
Delaware	Not enforced	One-parent notification (or counseling from grandparent or licensed mental health professional) with 24-hour waiting period or judicial bypass for minors under 16.	Life endangerment, rape, and incest only
District of Columbia	No	No	Life endangerment, rape, and incest only

(Continued)

State	Informed Consent/ Waiting Period	Parental Consent/ Notification	Medicaid Coverage
Florida	No	No	Life endangerment, rape, and incest only
Georgia	No	One-parent notification with 24-hour waiting period or judicial bypass	Life endangerment, rape, and incest only
Hawaii	No	No	Yes
Idaho	"If reasonably possible," women must receive state-mandated materials. 24-hour waiting period	"If reasonably possible," one-parent notification with 24-hour waiting period. No judicial bypass	Yes
Illinois	No	No	Yes
Indiana	No	One-parent consent or judicial bypass	Life endangerment, rape, and incest only
Iowa	No	One-parent notification or judicial bypass.	Life endangerment, rape, incest, and some cases of fetal deformity
Kansas	Women must receive state-mandated materials. 24-hour waiting period	One-parent notification or judicial bypass, and mandatory options counseling	Life endangerment, rape, and incest only
Kentucky	Not enforced	One-parent consent or judicial bypass	Life endangerment, rape, and incest only

Louisiana	State-mandated lecture and information. 24-hour waiting period and face-to-face session with doctor required	One-parent consent or judicial bypass	Life endangerment, rape, and incest only
Maine	No	Consent of one parent or adult family member, judicial bypass or options counseling from medical/mental health professional	Life endangerment, rape, and incest
Maryland	No	One-parent notification or physician bypass	Yes
Massachusetts	Not enforced	One-parent consent or judicial bypass	Yes
Michigan	Not enforced	One-parent consent or judicial bypass	Life endangerment, rape, and incest only
Minnesota	No	Two-parent notification with 48-hour waiting period or judicial bypass	Yes
Mississippi	Women must receive state-mandated lecture and materials. 24-hour waiting period and face-to-face session with doctor required	Two-parent consent or judicial bypass	Life endangerment only

(*Continued*)

State	Informed Consent/ Waiting Period	Parental Consent/ Notification	Medicaid Coverage
Missouri	No	One-parent consent or judicial bypass	Life endangerment, rape, and incest only
Montana	Not enforced	One-parent notification with 48-hour waiting period or judicial bypass	Yes
Nebraska	Women must receive state-mandated lecture and materials. 24-hour waiting period	One-parent notification with 48-hour waiting period or judicial bypass (declared unenforceable)	Life endangerment, rape, and incest only
Nevada	No	One-parent notification or judicial bypass (declared unenforceable)	Life endangerment, rape, and incest only
New Hampshire	No	No	Life endangerment, rape, and incest only
New Jersey	No	No	Yes
New Mexico	No	One-parent consent (declared unenforceable)	Yes
New York	No	No	Yes
North Carolina	No	One-parent consent (or grandparent with whom teen has been living for 6 mos) or judicial bypass	Life endangerment, rape, and incest only

North Dakota	Women must receive state-mandated lecture and materials. 24-hour waiting period	Two-parent consent or judicial bypass	Life endangerment, rape, and incest only
Ohio	Women must receive state-mandated lecture and materials. 24-hour waiting period	One-parent notification (or in some cases other adult family member) with 24-hour waiting period or judicial bypass	Life endangerment, rape, or incest
Oklahoma	No	No	Life endangerment, rape, and incest only
Oregon	No	No	Yes
Pennsylvania	Women must receive state-mandated lecture and materials. 24-hour waiting period and face-to-face session with doctor required	One-parent consent or judicial bypass	Life endangerment, rape, and incest only
Rhode Island	No	One-parent consent or judicial bypass	Life endangerment, rape, and incest only
South Carolina	Women must receive state-mandated materials. One-hour waiting period	One-parent/ grandparent consent or judicial bypass for unemancipated minors under 17	Life endangerment, rape, and incest only

(*Continued*)

State	Informed Consent/ Waiting Period	Parental Consent/ Notification	Medicaid Coverage
South Dakota	Women must receive state-mandated lecture and materials. 24-hour waiting period	One-parent notification or judicial bypass	Life endangerment only
Tennessee	Not enforced	One-parent consent with judicial bypass (declared unenforceable)	Life endangerment, rape, and incest only
Texas	No	No	Life endangerment, rape, and incest only
Utah	Women must receive state-mandated lecture and materials. 24-hour waiting period and face-to-face session with health professional required	Notification; no judicial bypass	Life endangerment, rape, and incest only
Virginia	No	One-parent notification with 24-hour waiting period or judicial bypass; physician bypass allowed in cases of sexual abuse	Life endangerment, rape, and incest only
Washington	No	No	Yes

West Virginia	No	One-parent notification with 24-hour waiting period, or physician or judicial bypass	Yes
Wisconsin	Not enforced	One-parent consent (or other family member over age 25) or judicial bypass	Life endangerment, rape, and incest only
Wyoming	No	One-parent consent with 48-hour waiting period or judicial bypass	Life endangerment, rape, or incest

What to Do if You Want to Continue Your Pregnancy

When I got pregnant, I said, "You know what? I can't do it this time. I just can't do another abortion." So I made a decision to have my daughter.

—NAOMI

Because this book is focused on abortion, this chapter provides only an overview of your options. It will walk you through your two alternatives for continuing your pregnancy—adoption and parenting—and guide you through the steps you'll need to take no matter what you decide. It is a good chapter to read even if you are not sure you want to continue your pregnancy.

If you haven't read Chapter One already, read it now. Chapter One gives information you'll need about how to take care of yourself during pregnancy, including how to deal with morning sickness and other symptoms of pregnancy and why it's important to avoid alcohol, drugs, and tobacco.

When I was pregnant with Alicia, I didn't have a test or anything, it was weird. I had a dream God said I was pregnant, he had long hair, blue eyes. In this dream all of us were pregnant, me, my friend, and my sister. And all three of us were.

—LAURA

Begin Prenatal Care

By ten weeks LMP (or sooner, if possible), you need to begin seeing a doctor regularly to make sure your pregnancy is healthy. Doctor visits during pregnancy are called prenatal care, and can make a huge difference in how well the pregnancy goes for you and your baby. Women who don't get prenatal care are more likely to have premature babies and more likely to have serious, even deadly, health problems. You'll find that your doctor, clinic, or county health department are very helpful when it comes to getting your prenatal care started. Don't wait!

PLAN FOR PAYING YOUR MEDICAL COSTS

The cash cost of prenatal care and childbirth range from an absolute low of a few thousand dollars to a high of over a million dollars, which can be the cost of a complicated pregnancy, birth, or both. There is no way to predict whether you will have a perfect pregnancy and a healthy birth, and for this reason health insurance is very important.

If you have health insurance, make sure it covers these costs and that you will have continuous coverage until well after the birth. If you are under the age of twenty-two, you might be covered under your parents' insurance (different plans have different age limits). These are questions that need to be worked out now.

If you don't have insurance, it may be difficult to get a policy that will cover your pregnancy. Pregnancy is considered a "preexisting condition" and many insurance companies will not cover your pregnancy-related costs if you were previously uninsured. If you buy your own insurance, expect to pay between $150 and $200 a month for it. If you are part of a school, workplace, or other organization, you may have access to group discounts.

If you are a teenager or you have a low income, you are probably eligible for free insurance through the federal Medicaid program. Even if you are working, Medicaid will often pay part of your health care expenses. Many communities also have other programs to provide free prenatal care. It is always worth checking whether this assistance is available to you. Your doctor or clinic can put you in touch with an eligibility worker. For a list of things you'll need to bring to meet with the eligibility worker, see "Medicaid" in Chapter Seven.

Remember, even if you have no insurance and no money, health care is available for your pregnancy and childbirth, even if it means showing up at the hospital emergency room. Don't let a lack of money stop you from getting the care you need and deserve.

Once you have a baby, there is no fun. Being a parent is gratifying but you have to think about someone before yourself, with everything you do. I was no longer Meg, I was Troy's mother.

—MEG

PARENTING

The subject of motherhood is so large it would take a whole library to give you all the important information. And if motherhood is your choice, it is strongly suggested that you go to the library rather than relying on this brief chapter. It is also suggested that you get all the help and teaching you can from friends who are parents. This section of the book deals mostly with financial considerations of parenthood, helping you to assess some of the steps you'll need to take to be prepared for the arrival of a baby.

Marriage Versus Single Motherhood

Everybody knows it is a whole lot easier to be a mother when there's another adult in the house to help out. This doesn't necessarily have to be a husband—it can be a boyfriend, girlfriend, parent, or friend. What's important is whether they are committed to your and your baby's support—including earning money, sharing in housework and child care, or being there for you both emotionally. If marriage is what you want from your male partner, now is the time to have that conversation. Marriage does not guarantee that he will support you, however. Again, it is his commitment that counts.

Without a partner, motherhood is certainly possible but it's very, very hard work, especially during the child's infancy. Half of all single mothers have incomes below the federal poverty line. If you work or go to school, you are going to need some adult support besides day care, period. Even a saint would get crazy from a life of all work and baby care.

If single motherhood is the route you choose, you'll have lots of company. As more and more women choose it (or get there because a marriage ends), the more single parents can stick together (the personal ads in some news weeklies these days even have special sections for single parents who want to meet each other).

Now is the time to get commitments from your partner, friends, and relatives about just how much help they will give you. Can you live with your parents for a while? Will your sister offer to baby-sit once week? Will your grandfather pay for your health insurance? Will your employer convert your job to a shared position so you can cut down to part-time? Is your partner willing to care for the baby on certain days? You cannot and should not try to do it all by yourself. Don't be afraid to ask for what you need, but be realistic about how well you expect these people to fulfill the commitments they make.

Maternity Leave and Disability

Most mothers who work take at least three months off from work after their baby is born. Some take more and some take less, and some take time off before the birth as well. As part of the Family and Medical Leave Act, some employers are required to hold jobs open for women on maternity leave until they can return. Check with your employer or your state labor department to see if you are eligible. Employers are not required to pay you during your leave.

If you work, you may be eligible for state disability payments during your maternity leave. You can get information about the procedure for getting disability payments, whether you are eligible, and how much you can expect by calling your state department of employment. Be warned that disability payments are usually much less than you earn at your job.

Child Support Payments

You are entitled to child support payments from your child's father even if he's not working and even if you marry someone else. The average child support payment is about $250 a month, depending on the incomes of the parents. States are passing tougher enforcement laws to get non-custodial parents (the ones who don't have custody) to pay the full amount of their court-ordered support, but most do not. To get child support payments, you will have to establish that your male partner is in fact the father. If he does not voluntarily admit he is the father, you can initiate a paternity suit. For information about this procedure, call your county district attorney's office.

Child Care

If you work, you will need child care. If this can't be provided for free by a friend or relative, child care will probably be the largest expense associated with your child. Costs vary in different communities throughout the country, but expect to pay about the same amount it would cost to rent a small one-bedroom apartment in your community. Just as rents vary from neighborhood to neighborhood, child care costs vary according to quality and other factors.

Long-Term Health Insurance

Having health insurance is extremely important for parents and their children, and it can be very hard to pay for. If you're receiving welfare or not working, you may qualify for Medicaid. Medicaid is the federal health insurance program for low-income families. If you have a low-paying job that does not provide health coverage for you and your dependents, however, you could be in a tough position. Many Americans are stuck between being eligible for Medicaid and being able to afford private health insurance. Unfortunately, there is no easy solution for you if this is your predicament.

What Does It Cost to Have a Child?

The following figures estimate the extra expenses you'll have with the birth of a child.

- Cost per month for middle-income family
  (cost rises as child ages)   about $621
- Cost per month, not counting
  child care and health care $410
- Cost over eighteen years $144,736

Source: "Cost of Raising a Child," 1995; Cutler, 1990 [figures adjusted for inflation].

Government Funding for Mothers and Children

Government funds are sometimes available for low-income mothers. The recent reform of the welfare system has changed a lot of the rules, but here's the basic information.

- Welfare used to be called AFDC, but now it's called TANF. This stands for "temporary assistance to needy families" and people pronounce it "tanniff."

- Welfare used to come from the U.S. government but now it comes from your state government.

- Your state can make a lot of its own rules about who gets it and how much. For this reason, you should call your county offices to find out if you are eligible and what rules apply.

- Welfare payments average less than $400 a month. Payments vary a lot by state, so it could be a lot less than this.

- You are now required to start working within two years of receiving welfare. Some counties have programs to help you with job training and child care, though these programs are not always very good. Some states will let you go to vocational school for one year instead of working for that year.

- There is now a lifetime limit of five years for receiving welfare. If you get welfare for five years, does this mean the state will let you starve to death? Not necessarily. States may give welfare to certain families for longer periods of time.

- If you are under eighteen and unmarried, you'll have to live with your parents or in some other adult-supervised situation in order to get TANF.

- Food stamps may be available to poor families in addition to TANF. Legal immigrants can no longer get food stamps.

- Medicaid (called MediCal in California) is health insurance for people on TANF. Even if you are no longer eligible for TANF, you may still be eligible for Medicaid.

- States can now take stronger actions to get your male partner to pay child support (but don't count on receiving child support payments).

- All these programs have complicated procedures and paperwork for the people who want them, so get started early on the application process.

- Your doctor or clinic can tell you who to call or visit to get started (Children's Defense Fund).

Crisis Pregnancy Centers

If you're absolutely sure you want to continue your pregnancy, one option for support is a crisis pregnancy center. You can find them in the

Yellow Pages under "Abortion Alternatives." Some will give you free counseling and help you apply for government funding available for pregnant women. Some will also give you free baby clothes and furniture, help you find a place to live while you are pregnant, or connect you with adoption agencies.

If there's still a possibility that you will choose abortion, it would be best to steer clear of these centers, as their whole purpose is to try to stop women from having abortions. To do this, they show their clients films and give lectures—materials that sometimes give false information designed to scare you out of having an abortion. For more information, see "How to Avoid Fake Clinics" in Chapter Seven).

If You're a Teen

When I counsel pregnant teenagers who are leaning toward parenting, I often find they have unrealistic ideas about babies, their future, and their male partner. "I know my boyfriend's going to be there for me," these girls will typically assure me. "I'm pretty sure we'll get married and have a nice house." The short time period during which girls must decide about their pregnancies is no time for denial and vagueness.

Eighty percent of teens who have babies drop out of high school. Those who don't usually have strong family support and child care. Most cities have programs that provide child care while teen mothers attend adult school, but completion is rare. If you're thinking about becoming a mom, ask yourself honestly if you have the family support and self-discipline to devote almost all your waking hours to classes, studies, and caring for a baby.

No matter what your boyfriend says, you should know that relationships between teen mothers and their male partners almost never last, no matter how good the relationship is now. Girls should never count on support from their male partner. Precious few even participate financially in the child's life, even though they are required to by law.

Welfare, food stamps, and Medicaid will cover medical and some living expenses for some teens and their children for a lifetime total of five years. With new welfare reform laws, teen mothers must live with their parents or in approved, adult-supervised situations and they must go to high school until they turn eighteen or graduate. All mothers who receive welfare must start working and at least partially support themselves within two years. It is somewhat unlikely when the time is up that you will be able to support yourself and your child without outside support. Family support is essential; commitments from family members should be obtained now, while you still have options about your pregnancy.

Now, with all that negative stuff out of the way, here is the positive side. Many teen mothers say that having a baby was the best thing that ever happened to them. These mothers are comfortable with the hard work required and with the limitations on their social life. Some say having a baby gave them a focus and helped them get their lives together. If having a baby is your choice, and if you're committed enough, you can make your life a success.

> *I had to give one baby up for adoption. It was too late by the time I knew I was pregnant to have an abortion. I didn't want to see or hear or smell that baby. I just said "take it away." I would never do that adoption thing again.*
>
> —RITA

> *I considered adoption, but I didn't think I could do it. I was a very smart and sensitive kid and I didn't want my kid to be smashed down for that, the way I was. With adoption I wouldn't have any control. On the other hand, I feared that if I raised the child I'd raise it as badly as I was raised.*
>
> —LISA

ADOPTION

Almost three out of every hundred women facing an unintended pregnancy ends up choosing adoption. Although we usually think of adoption as the placing of a child with strangers, nearly half of all adoptions are to relatives.

Many women who chose adoption will tell you it was the hardest choice they could have made, but for most of them it was the only choice that felt right. Many women who seek information about placing their babies for adoption don't end up going through with it, but say they feel better having explored all their options.

Unlike abortion and parenting, adoption in most states requires permission from the woman's male partner. If he does not consent the adoption often can still be approved, but it involves going to court. If he wishes to raise the child himself and is approved by the court as a suitable parent, some judges will block adoption proceedings.

Some adoptions are handled by state agencies, some by nonprofit or religious organizations, and some privately by attorneys. In the past, all adoptions were "closed," meaning records of the birth mother's identity and the child's identity were kept secret from the public and from each other. In recent years, long-separated mothers and children have searched for each other, been reunited, and, in many cases, started a new relationship.

More and more states now permit "open" adoption, where birth mothers (and sometimes fathers) choose the adoptive parents and may keep an ongoing relationship with them and the child after the adoption takes place. Open adoption is still confidential—even the birth mother's parents do not have to be informed that the adoption or even the birth has taken place. The agency does not disclose identities to anyone but the birth mother and the adoptive parents.

In open adoption, it is now customary for the adoptive parents to pay the medical and living expenses of the birth mother for the duration of her pregnancy. And though birth mothers normally maintain contact with adoptive families—and choose families who agree on how much contact is appropriate—this agreement is not legally binding.

In open adoptions and those handled in certain agencies, infants can be placed with adoptive parents as soon as they are born. This can be an advantage over many closed agency adoptions where infants must first be placed in foster care while prospective adoptive parents are investigated.

All birth mothers express some sadness about their decision to place their children for adoption, even though most feel it was the best decision. There are some women, unfortunately, who deeply regret placing their children for adoption. There is little research about how birth mothers fare over time, but women with regrets are likely to be those who felt pressured—either by their own friends and family or by the adoptive parents, attorney, or agency. Unlike the situation with abortion and parenting, other people have much to gain from the adoption taking place, not just the adoptive parents. Attorneys and agencies earn money from the transaction, and their vested interest in the adoption going through could translate to pressure. To avoid pressure, birth mothers are advised to retain their own attorney separate from any who work for the adoptive parents and to obtain counseling outside any agencies that make placements or in any way serve adoptive parents.

Until the birth mother signs adoption papers giving up her rights as a parent, she can change her mind. This is always done after the birth of the baby, but the number of days varies by state. You should not sign anything before this point.

Adoption is far more common among white people than among people of color. Healthy white babies are usually easily adopted, but nonwhite and disabled babies can end up spending months or even years in foster care. For African-American babies especially, adoptive families are not always available.

For information on open adoption call the Independent Adoption Center at 1-800-877-OPEN. For referrals to licensed adoption agencies (open and closed), contact the National Committee for Adoption hotline at 1-202-328-8072. If you are pregnant you can call collect. For information about private adoption, look in the Yellow Pages under "Attorneys, Family Law."

How to Heal After the Abortion: Write-In Section

Once the crisis of the unintended pregnancy is over, the pressure is off and there is more room for quiet feelings and thoughts. The days and weeks following an abortion are a time for healing. Physically, the strong hormones of pregnancy return to normal and symptoms disappear. Nausea leaves, appetite and energy return, and the emotional intensity of the pregnancy begins to lighten.

Our feelings about our decision may be simple. Most of us felt relieved, glad the experience was over, and hopeful that we would never have to go through this again. But if there were any lingering feelings of doubt or guilt, we had some work to do. These were not feelings that had to burden us for the rest of our lives. We could face our feelings, make what amends we could, and become free of any negativity surrounding our decision.

Even if we felt good about our decision, it could help to review the experience of our pregnancy and abortion, and to say with clarity: yes, we did the right thing.

THE PHYSICAL ABORTION EXPERIENCE

Pregnancy was a powerful physical experience. Some of us quickly returned to our normal state, and others gradually lost the symptoms of pregnancy. The abortion itself was for many of us an equally intense physical experience, made stronger sometimes by what we were feeling inside.

- Overall, what was it like for you to be pregnant? Did you have positive feelings about it?

_____

_____

_____

- If you hope to have a planned pregnancy someday, how do you imagine it will be different from this experience?

_____

_____

_____

- Was your abortion physically painful?

_____

- Is the pregnant feeling gone now? What do you feel like now?

_____

- How are you taking care of yourself to promote your physical healing after the abortion?

_____

_____

_____

- How do you feel about your body today?

_____

THE EMOTIONAL ABORTION EXPERIENCE

An unintended pregnancy was already a crisis for many of us, but together with hormonal changes the whole experience could be overwhelming. After the abortion things usually calmed down, and we had time to reflect on our feelings.

- Looking back, what were the strongest feelings you had throughout your pregnancy?

_____

_____

_____

- What were your feelings during the abortion?

_____

_____

_____

- What were your feelings immediately after the abortion? Have those feelings changed?

_____

_____

_____

- Did having an abortion change you?

_____

- What positive things have come about because of this experience?

_____

_____

- Have any negative things happened because of this experience?

_____

_____

_____

- Do you have thoughts and feelings about the potential child that was aborted?

_____

_____

_____

- What are your feelings today about your relationship with your male partner?

_____

_____

_____

In Good Conscience

- Are there any feelings that are bothering you at this point? What do you need, or what can you do, to feel better?

_____

_____

_____

THE SPIRITUAL ABORTION EXPERIENCE

For some of us, touching our capacity to create life gave us a powerful connection to our spirituality. Some of us probed the hard questions— Was this pregnancy a life? Was it a spirit? Do spirits exist before life, or after life on earth? Is there reincarnation? Did we choose what was best?

Facing these questions was sometimes frightening and sometimes painful but ultimately it deepened our consciousness. Many of us came through the abortion experience with a stronger sense of purpose in life, as though we'd been given a second chance.

- Do you feel a connection with a power greater than yourself?

_____

- Did you feel such a connection during your abortion experience? If so, what was that like?

_____

_____

_____

• How do you seek a connection with your Higher Power?

_____

_____

_____

• What does this Higher Power want for you?

_____

_____

_____

• How does your Higher Power communicate with you? Did you receive any signs to guide your decision?

_____

_____

_____

• How do you think your Higher Power views your decision to have an abortion?

_____

_____

_____

In Good Conscience

- Do you have spiritual thoughts about the potential child that was aborted? What are your beliefs?

_____

_____

_____

- If you could communicate something to that potential being, what would you say?

_____

_____

_____

- Do you feel any guilt about choosing abortion? What can you do to "set things right"?

_____

_____

_____

HOW SUPPORT PEOPLE CAME THROUGH

Like other crises in life, our pregnancy put some of our relationships to the test. Some of us found renewed love and depth with our support people. Others of us were disappointed when those we trusted let us down and relationships we once relied upon appeared to fall away. It was important to acknowledge the love and help we did receive, even when it was not from those we had hoped. In the end, it was this kind of love that showed us we really are cared for, and that we really can survive even the hardest situations.

- With whom did you end up sharing your decision process?

_____

_____

_____

- Who was most helpful to you? How did this affect you?

_____

_____

_____

- Was anyone hurtful to you? How did they let you down?

_____

_____

_____

- Were you satisfied with the support of the clinic staff? How were they helpful? Were they hurtful to you in any way?

_____

_____

_____

- Who in your life now is available to support you in healing from your abortion experience?

_____

_____

_____

GOALS FOR HEALTHY SEXUALITY AND RELATIONSHIPS

Some of us had made mistakes that led to our unintended pregnancy. When we looked back at the way our sex life had been, we often saw there were changes we wanted to make. Many of us felt that somehow we had not been acting out of our best self or for our highest good. Perhaps we were having sex that did not feel right to us. Perhaps we were with partners with whom we could not be ourselves. Some of us felt that we had to hide our sexuality or pretend that we were "swept away" by surprise rather than appear to our male partners as though we were expecting sex. How our partner reacted to our pregnancy—if we felt we could tell him about it at all—also taught us much about our relationship with him.

- How was the quality of support from your male partner? What did he do well? Were there any ways he let you down?

_____

_____

_____

_____

- If you had it to do all over again, are there ways that you would have related to your partner differently throughout this experience?

_____

_____

_____

_____

- How would you like your relationship with your male partner to be, now that the abortion is over?

_____

_____

_____

- Do you and your partner share the same vision for your relationship? What are the similarities? What are the differences?

_____

_____

_____

_____

In Good Conscience

• What is your ideal—the best possible relationship you can imagine for yourself?

_____

_____

_____

GOALS FOR PREVENTION OF FUTURE UNINTENDED PREGNANCIES

Our pregnancy and abortion sometimes brought up strong feelings about our personal responsibility, and sometimes we felt the need to make resolutions for the future. Many of us felt sure that we did not want the same thing to happen again and swore we'd protect ourselves better, or be more careful, or leave our relationship, or never have sex again! Some of our resolutions were unrealistic—overreactions from negative thoughts. We looked for realistic ways to care for ourselves, knowing that sex and love would almost certainly be part of our lives once again.

• How will you protect yourself from future unplanned pregnancies?

_____

_____

_____

• Do you expect to be sexually active in the coming year?

_____

- If so, does your partner agree with you about what birth control to use?

  _____

- If you don't plan to be sexually active, how can you be prepared to prevent pregnancies when the time for sex returns?

  _____

- When do you think would be good time for a planned pregnancy in your life? How would you like your life to be at that time?

  _____

  _____

  _____

EXERCISES

1. Write a letter to the clinic staff or to a staff member who was particularly helpful to you. Express your thanks.

2. Write thank-you cards for those who helped you. Tell them of your love and gratitude.

3. Call a friend who is a single mother. Think of what she may need but doesn't have—a night out without the kids, movie tickets, a shoulder rub, a bag of groceries, some kind words. Give it to her!

4. Think of the children in your life. Think about what they need but don't have—someone to read to them, a trip to a restaurant or museum, a new pair of shoes, reassuring words, help with homework. Give it to them!

5. Meditation: in prayer, ask, How shall I bring greater goodness to my romantic relationships with people, including friends? Sit quietly for twenty minutes with eyes closed, allowing your mind to rest. Listen for wisdom from your Higher Power.

How to Use the Morning After Pill

The morning after pill—officially known as emergency contraception—is used after unprotected sex to help prevent pregnancy. The pills are ordinary birth control pills, which are available only with a doctor's prescription. Scientists believe that the pills work by preventing the fertilized egg from implanting into the wall of the uterus.

Emergency contraception must be started within seventy-two hours (three days) after unprotected sex. The sooner you start, the more effective they are. Side effects sometimes include nausea (half of all women who take it) and vomiting (one in five women), so it is not a good method for birth control every month. It is safe to take on a repeated basis, however. Emergency contraception is not guaranteed to prevent pregnancy; about one in four women who take it become pregnant anyway.

Brands of Birth Control Pills Approved for Use as Emergency Contraception: How to Use Them

Lo-Ovral	Take 4, repeat in 12 hours
Nordette	Take 4, repeat in 12 hours
Levlen	Take 4, repeat in 12 hours
Tri-Levlen (yellow pills)	Take 4, repeat in 12 hours
Tri-Phasil (yellow pills)	Take 4, repeat in 12 hours
Ovral	Take 2, repeat in 12 hours

You can get more information by calling the Emergency Contraceptive Hotline at 1-800-584-9911.

For Men: Your Rights and Responsibilities

If you share responsibility for an unintended pregnancy, you may be in a difficult position. Although there is the possibility that you will be seriously affected by the woman's decision, you don't legally have a say in that decision. Furthermore, if she decides to have the baby and raise it without you, she is entitled to child support payments until the child turns eighteen. It is important to accept her role as the decision maker right now and to give her as much emotional support as you can. If you have feelings that conflict with hers about the pregnancy, it is okay to let her know how you feel, but not to pressure or blame her, just as it is inappropriate for her to blame you. If your feelings conflict, it is best that you find at least one other person other than her in whom you can confide.

The most loving thing you can do now is offer your support and step back when your help—or your opinions—are not desired. The quality of your support at this time is likely to have a large bearing on the future of your relationship. Even if you don't plan to continue the relationship, your loving support will make this event much easier for her.

If She Decides to Have an Abortion

If she chooses to have an abortion, it is appropriate (but not legally required) that you pay at least half of all costs. Most clinics will also allow the man to be present during the abortion procedure if it is what the woman wishes.

If She Decides to Parent

During your partner's pregnancy you don't have rights concerning her decision, but upon the birth of the child you begin to have father's rights. If you want to play an ongoing and active role in the child's life, your rights include the following.

1. The right to visit the child

2. The right to go to court to contest for custody of the child (but not necessarily the right to have custody)

3. The right to agree to or, in most states, to deny an adoption

4. The right to declare yourself as the father on the child's birth certificate

As the father, you also have the responsibility to provide financially for the child until he or she turns eighteen. This is called child support, and the mother can take you to court to establish how much you have to pay. If you do not pay child support or communicate with the child for at least one year you lose all your rights as a father, but you never can be free of your responsibility for the child's financial support. Fathers under the age of eighteen have the same responsibility as adults; this responsibility does not pass on to your parents. You have to pay this money whether or not you are working, whether or not you move to another state than the child, and whether or not the mother works, earns money, or remarries. Even when you have no money, you owe child support. Although in the past most fathers ordered by the court to pay child support have not paid the full amount owed over the years, these laws are now being enforced more strongly as part of welfare reform. The court can force you to pay by withholding money from your wages and income tax returns. They can also revoke your driver's license, professional licenses, and, in some cases, recreational licenses.

The mother also has the right to contest your rights—to use the court system to try to keep you from visiting or having custody of the child. She can also file a paternity suit to prove that you are or are not the father. In a paternity suit, if you deny that you are the father the court can order you to have a DNA blood test that can prove with 99.9 percent accuracy whether the child is yours. If you refuse to take the test or if you don't show up for the paternity suit, the court may find you to be the father. You can also file a paternity suit to prove that you are or are not the father.

For information and assistance regarding paternity suits and child support, contact your district court or district attorney's office.

If She Wishes to Place the Child for Adoption

Different states have very different adoption laws, but most require that the father sign the adoption papers as well as the mother. In these states the adoption can proceed if the father signs either permission for the adoption, a form denying he is the father, *or* a form stating he gives up his rights to the child. In "closed" adoption, the father then loses all rights to see or know the child forever. Some "open" adoption arrangements, however, permit fathers to remain involved in the child's life through contact with the adoptive family.

Some fathers wishing to have custody have filed suit against mothers who wish to place the child for adoption. If you and your partner are facing conflict about her decision to place the child for adoption, contact an adoption agency or attorney immediately. For more information, call the Independent Adoption Center, 1-800-877-OPEN, or the National Committee for Adoption, 1-202-328-8072.

Fetal Development

These illustrations show the approximate size of a fetus at several stages of pregnancy. Weeks given are weeks after last menstrual period (LMP). For more information on this topic, see Chapter Two.

4 weeks LMP

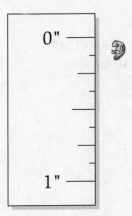

6 weeks LMP

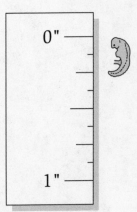

8 weeks LMP
(Actual size)

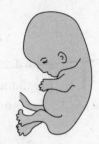

10 weeks LMP
(Actual size)

12 weeks LMP
(Actual size)

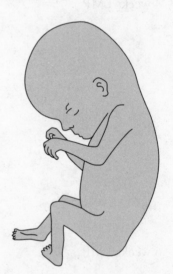

14 weeks LMP

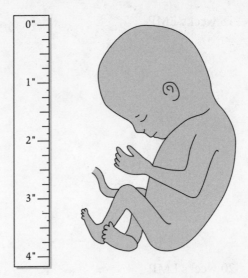

16 weeks LMP

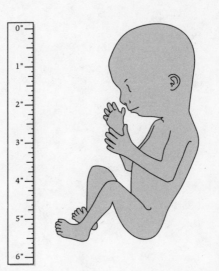

18 weeks LMP

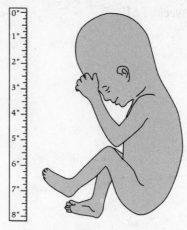

20 weeks LMP

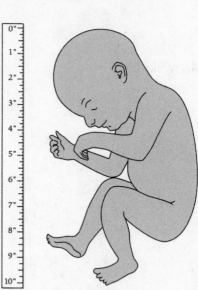

22 weeks LMP

28 weeks LMP

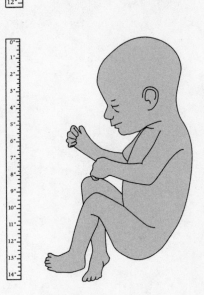

How to Learn More

Following is a summary of information sources listed in this book, plus a list of recommended books.

Helpful Phone Numbers

- For information and appointments, whether you continue your pregnancy or choose abortion, contact Planned Parenthood.
  1-800-230-PLAN
  http://www.plannedparenthood.org

- For information on abortion and abortion providers, contact the National Abortion Federation.
  1-800-772-9100
  http://www.prochoice.org/naf.

- For adoption information, call the Independent Adoption Center.
  1-800-877-OPEN
  Or call the National Committee for Adoption.
  (202) 328-8072

- For information on religion and abortion, call the Religious Coalition for Reproductive Choice.
  (202) 628-7700

- For information on the morning after pill, call the Emergency Contraceptive Hotline.
  1-800-584-9911

Helpful Books

The Abortion Resource Handbook by K. Kaufman (Simon & Schuster, 1997). A great resource on restrictive laws and other abortion-related information.

The Healing Choice: Your Guide to Emotional Recovery After Abortion by Candace De Puy and Dana Dovitch (Simon & Schuster, 1997).

The New Our Bodies, Ourselves by the Boston Women's Health Book Collective (Simon & Schuster, 1984). Everything you ever wanted to know about women's health.

Planned Parenthood's Women's Health Encyclopedia (Crown Trade Paperbacks, 1996). A modern and concise resource on women's health.

References

Note: Unless otherwise noted, all citations are from fact sheets of the Planned Parenthood Federation of America, 1988–1996, or the Alan Guttmacher Institute, 1988–1998.

Children's Defense Fund. "Summary of the New Welfare Legislation (Public Law 104-193)." Children's Defense Fund, Oct. 22, 1997.

Congressional Quarterly. "Welfare Reform Agreement, Conference Summary." House Action Reports, No. 104-15. July 30, 1996.

"Cost of Raising a Child." *Contra Costa Times* (Calif.), Jan. 22, 1995.

Cutler, B. "Rock-A-Buy Baby." *American Demographics,* Jan. 1990.

Henshaw, S. K., and Kost, K. "Abortion Patients in 1994–95: Characteristics and Contraceptive Use." *Family Planning Perspectives, 28,* 1996.

Independent Adoption Center. "Fact Sheet: Adoption in the United States." Independent Adoption Center (n.d.).

Kaufman, K. *The Abortion Resource Handbook.* New York: Fireside, 1997.

Lindsay, J. W. *Teen Dads: Rights, Responsibilities & Joys.* Buena Park, Calif: Morning Glory Press, 1993.

Luker, K. *Abortion and the Politics of Motherhood.* Berkeley: University of California Press, 1984.

Major, B. "Beyond Choice: Myths and Facts About Adjustment to Abortion." California Wellness Foundation/University of California Wellness Lecture Series, 1997.

National Abortion Rights Action League Foundation. *Who Decides: A State-by-State Review of Abortion and Reproductive Rights.*: National Abortion Rights Action League, 1998 (photocopied).

Planned Parenthood Association of San Mateo County. *If You Get Someone Pregnant* (brochure). San Mateo, Calif.: Planned Parenthood Association of San Mateo County, 1991.

Religious Coalition for Reproductive Choice. *Religious Organizations' Statements on Reproductive Choice.* Washington, D.C.: Religious Coalition for Reproductive Choice, June, 1996.

Religious Coalition for Reproductive Choice. *Speakout #1.* Washington, D.C.: Religious Coalition for Reproductive Choice, 1995 (photocopied).

Russo, N. F. "Psychological Aspects of Unwanted Pregnancy and its Resolution." *Family Planning Perspectives,* 1987, *19*(2), 76–77.

Russo, N. F., and Horn, J. D. "Unwanted Pregnancy and Its Resolution: Options, Implications." In J. Freeman (ed.), *Women: A Feminist Perspective.* Mountain View, Calif.: Mayfield, 1995.

Silber, K., and Speedlin, P. *Dear Birthmother.* San Antonio: Corona, 1991.

Index

Insurance. *See* Health insurance
Invasive procedures, 30

J

Jewish Women International, 72
Judicial bypass, 111
Judgement, 6

K

Kaufman, K., 112, 158
Kost, K., 9, 10, 11

L

Laminaria, 27, 29
Laws, restricting abortion, 110, 112
Laws, by state, 113–119
Legality, of abortion, 66, 67
Levlen, 145
Life goals, 88–89
LMP (Last Menstrual Period), calculating, 13–14, 18, 23, 28, 122
Lo-Ovral, 145
Luker, K., 66
Lutheran Women's Caucus, 72

M

Major, B., 10, 32, 33
Male partner: consent of, in adoption, 130, 149; feelings about, 90–92; rights and responsibilities of, in unintended pregnancy, 147–149
Manual aspiration, 28–29, 31
Marriage, sacredness of, 68–69
Maternity leave, 124–125
Medicaid, 19, 103, 104, 123, 125–126, 127, 128
Medicaid eligibility worker, 103
MediCal, 103, 127
Medical costs, paying for, 122–123
Medical method(non-surgical), 29–30
Men: and child support, 148–149; and cost of abortion, 147; feelings about, 90–91; and placement for adoption, 149; rights and responsibilities of, in unintended pregnancy, 147–149
Methotrexate, 30

Midwifes, 66–67
Mifepristone, 29, 30
Miscarriage, waiting for, versus choosing abortion, 17
Misoprostol, 29–30
Moravian Church in America, Northern Province, 72
Morning after pill, 145
Morning sickness, 16
Motherhood. *See* Parenting
Myths, about abortion: and breast cancer, 32; and permanent psychological damage, 32; and sterility, 31–32

N

NA'AMAT USA, 72
Narcotics Anonymous, 16
National Abortion Federation, 104, 105, 106, 112, 157
National Abortion Rights Action League, 113
National Committee for Adoption, 131, 149, 157
National Council of Jewish Women, 72
New Our Bodies, Ourselves, The (Boston Women's Health Book Collective), 158
Nordette, 145
North American Federation of Temple Youth, 72

O

Open adoption, 130–131, 149
Organized religion, and abortion, 7, 11, 66–67, 70–73
Ovral, 145

P

Parental consent and notification, 110–111
Parenting: and child care, 125; and child support payments, 125; and crisis pregnancy centers, 127–128; and government funding for mothers and children, 126–127; and long-term health insurance, 125–126; and marriage, versus single motherhood, 123–124; and maternity leave and disability, 124–125; and teen mothers, 128–129

U

Ultrasound imaging, 14, 23, 24
Unintended pregnancies, 2–3, 7, 8, 143–144
Union of American Hebrew Congregations, 71, 72
Unitarian Universalist Association, 71, 72
United Church of Christ, 71, 72
United Methodist Church, 71, 72
United Synagogue for Conservative Judaism, 71, 72
Unprotected sex, 76, 92, 145

V

Vacuum aspiration, 28, 31

W

Wade, Roe v., 67
Waiting period requirements, 112
Welfare, 126, 128
Women of Reform Judaism, 72
Women's American ORT, 73
Women's League of Conservative Judaism, 73

Y

Yellow pages, 105, 127–128, 131
Young Women's Christian Association of the United States, 73